NEUROPSYCHOLOGY
FOR OCCUPATIONAL THERAPISTS

Assessment of Perception and Cognition

JUNE GRIEVE BSc, MSc

OXFORD

BLACKWELL SCIENTIFIC PUBLICATIONS

LONDON EDINBURGH BOSTON

MELBOURNE PARIS BERLIN VIENNA

© June Grieve 1993

Blackwell Scientific Publications
Editorial Offices:
Osney Mead, Oxford OX2 0EL
25 John Street, London WC1N 2BL
23 Ainslie Place, Edinburgh EH3 6AJ
238 Main Street, Cambridge,
    Massachusetts, 02142, USA
54 University Street, Carlton,
    Victoria 3053, Australia

Other Editorial Offices:
Librairie Arnette SA
2, rue Casimir-Delavigne
75006 Paris
France

Blackwell Wissenschafts-Verlag GmbH
Meinekestrasse 4
D-1000 Berlin 15
Germany

Blackwell MZV
Feldgasse 13
A-1238 Wien
Austria

First published 1993

Set by DP Photosetting, Aylesbury, Bucks
Printed and bound in Great Britain by
Hartnolls Ltd, Bodmin, Cornwall

DISTRIBUTORS

Marston Book Services Ltd
PO Box 87
Oxford OX2 0DT
(*Orders*: Tel: 0865 791155
        Fax: 0865 791927
        Telex: 837515)

USA
Blackwell Scientific Publications, Inc.
238 Main Street
Cambridge, MA 02142
(*Orders*: Tel: 800 759-6102
        617 876-7000)

Canada
Times Mirror Professional Publishing, Ltd
130 Flaska Drive
Markham, Ontario L6G 1B8
(*Orders*: Tel: 800 268-4178)
        416 470-6739)

Australia
Blackwell Scientific Publications Pty Ltd
54 University Street
Carlton, Victoria 3053
(*Orders*: Tel: 03 347-5552)

British Library
Cataloguing in Publication Data

A catalogue record for this title
is available from the British Library

ISBN 0–632–03303-7

Library of Congress
Cataloging in Publication Data

Grieve, June I.
    Neuropsychology for occupational therapists:
    assessment of perception and cognition/June Grieve.
    Includes bibliographical references and index.
    ISBN 0 632 03303 7
    1. Neuropsychological tests.   2. Clinical
neuropsychology.   3. Occupational therapy.
4. Occupational therapists.   I. Title.
    [DNLM: 1 Neuropsychology.   2. Brain—
physiopathology.   3. Perception—physiology.
4. Cognition—physiology.   5. Occupational Therapy.
WL 103 G848n 1993]
RC386.6.N48G75   1993
616.8′0475—dc20
                                        93-19447
                                        CIP

Contents

Foreword

In the light of an increasing elderly population, and the increase in the number of young people that survive traumatic head injury, it now becomes more important for occupational therapists to be aware of the many complex and disabling deficits that may result following brain damage. In order to focus on the areas of perception and cognition, this book has not covered behavioural, psychosocial, intellectual or motor ability – though the importance of these aspects should not be overlooked in the successful rehabilitation of neurologically impaired patients.

The brain is a very complex system and identical lesions in two different patients may result in different functional problems. Therefore it is unrealistic to provide concrete recipes for the assessment of disorders based on a diagnostic approach. Occupational therapists are appropriate interventionists because they view the patient holistically in addressing functional problems, and do not concentrate purely on the disorder itself.

There are increasing pressures on clinicians to minimize their input for financial reasons. It is now becoming imperative that occupational therapists can assess patients competently and professionally, and present their reasons for the patient requiring more, not less, intervention. This is difficult in a health service that is more focused on overt physical signs of dysfunction, and less interested in the often hidden symptoms of patients with perceptual or cognitive dysfunction.

This book is aimed at students and experienced clinicians who want to acquire confidence in assessing patients' deficits following neurological damage, based on an understanding of the underlying mechanisms.

The book content includes the anatomy of the brain, and the deficits resulting from particular lesion sites. Both objective and subjective tools and materials are described for testing the resulting deficits. Clinicians will be given a good starting point for the correlation of neurology with problems in functional tasks. For the purpose of completing the book, the author has taken a purist approach and looked at each deficit in isolation from others, so that these areas could be considered in some depth. However, the clinician must never lose sight of the complexities of the brain, and the fact that the patient may often present with multiple problems.

Jacqueline Adams
Dip COT, OTR

Preface

This book is written for students preparing to enter the paramedical professions, and for clinicians involved in the rehabilitation of patients with neurological impairment. The undergraduate student of occupational therapy will find an integration of theory and practice for the assessment of perception and cognition. Experienced clinicians working in acute rehabilitation and community settings will be encouraged to include more in-depth assessment of perceptual and cognitive deficits in the functional assessment of their clients.

Neuroanatomical and information processing approaches to understanding perception and cognition are used. The reader is encouraged to develop an awareness of how perception and cognition affect function in self-care, work and leisure activities, and to predict the effects of impairment.

The areas covered in the book are mainly relevant to occupational therapy and language disorders are not included. Standardized test batteries for the assessment of perception and cognition are summarized.

Part I serves as an introduction to the methods of neuropsychology and cognitive neuropsychology, and to the role of perception and cognition in daily living.

Part II outlines the theoretical background to knowledge of perceptual and cognitive abilities under the following headings: visual perception and object recognition; spatial abilities; action planning and sequencing; attention; and memory. Activities are given which help the reader acquire experience of perceptual and cognitive function.

Part III describes perceptual and cognitive deficits under the same headings as Part II. Each deficit is defined and the functional implications are considered. Suggestions are listed for the assessment of each deficit, including the relevant component tests from standardized assessment batteries.

June Grieve

Acknowledgements

I am indebted to all the occupational therapists, many of them my former students, who have helped me to integrate the theoretical knowledge with their clinical experience. In particular, Jacqueline Adams has given me continuous support and expert opinion throughout the preparation of this book. Many of the suggestions for activities to develop awareness of the role of perception and cognition in daily living were devised by her and Tina Rollafson for a College of Occupational Therapy post-registration course. Helen Brown contributed helpful comments for the chapters on memory. Special thanks are also given to Jo Creighton who devised and produced the original drawings in Parts I and II, and to Maggie Walker for the cover design.

David Sanchez created the original drawings in Part III, and Samantha Wilcox produced the diagrams of the brain.

Richard Miles and Lisa Field of Blackwell Scientific Publications have maintained a professional and cheerful stimulus for my endeavour. Caroline Savage has patiently worked with me on the preparation of the manuscript for press.

Finally, the book would not have been written without the constant support of my family, Don, John and Ann, who have helped me in too many ways to mention.

Extracts from the Rivermead Perceptual Assessment Battery © J. Whiting, N. Lincoln, G. Bhavnani & J. Cockburn, 1985 are included by permission of the publishers, NFER-NELSON. Extracts from the Chessington Occupational Therapy Assessment Battery are included by permission of Nottingham Rehab Ltd. The extract from the Behavioural Inattention Test is included by permission of Thames Valley Test Company.

Part I Theoretical Approaches to Perception and Cognition

Chapter 1   Introduction to Neuropsychology

Neuropsychology has grown out of the convergence of the medical science of neurology and psychology in the common study of the behavioural effects of brain damage. The methodology of cognitive psychology is incorporated into the study of impaired cognitive systems in cognitive neuropsychology, which emerged as a related discipline in the 1970s. Over the same period, there has been a large increase in the number of studies of cognitive function in neuropsychology. All the disciplines involved in the study of perpetual and cognitive function are summarized in Fig. 1.1.

1.1 Approaches in neuropsychology

1.1.1 Localization

The localization view in neuropsychology analyses mental processing in the brain into independent components of perception and action. Cerebral damage is interpreted in terms of the loss of a specific component, or the disconnection of interaction between separate

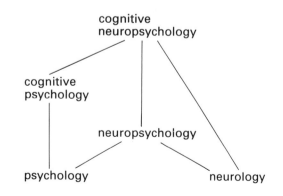

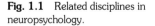
Fig. 1.1   Related disciplines in neuropsychology.

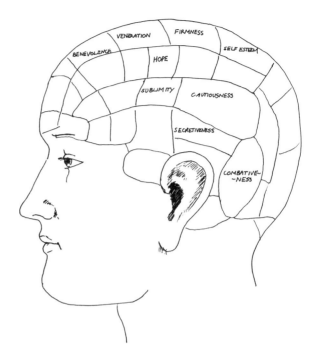

Fig. 1.2   Gall's phrenological map.

components. A simple analogy with a car would be that engine failure is due to damage of one of the parts of the engine, or to one of the electrical or mechanical connections between them. The features of the engine failure will depend on which part or connection is disrupted.

The phrenologists, in the early nineteenth century, were the first to suggest that the brain was divided into 'organs' or faculties with different intellectual and emotional functions, such as cautiousness, hope, self-esteem, see Fig. 1.2.

Gall, and his many followers, believed that a highly developed faculty indicated a correspondingly large area in the cerebral cortex, and that this was revealed in the head as a bump in the skull overlying it.

Later in the same century, the post mortem examination of patients with known deficits identified areas of the cerebral hemispheres concerned with the production of speech (Broca's area), and receptive aspects of speech and language (Wernicke's area), see Fig. 1.3. These discoveries were also the first to localize language functions in the left hemisphere.

Early animal experiments in neurophysiology used electrical stimulation of the surface of the brain to demonstrate that localized areas of the surface of the brain produced movements in the opposite side of the body. Penfield, a Canadian neurosurgeon, explored the surface of the brain of patients with severe epilepsy in an attempt to find the focus of the seizure. Areas for vision, hearing, body sensation and

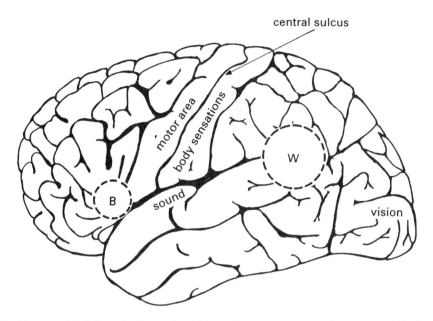

Fig. 1.3   Side view of the left cerebral hemisphere showing the primary motor and sensory areas. B – Broca's area, W – Wernicke's area.

movement were identified, in particular lobes of the cerebral hemispheres, see Fig. 1.3. These techniques have been used to localize the primary sensory and motor areas in the brain, but cannot be used to investigate complex cognitive functions.

The development of brain imaging techniques over recent years means that the sites of brain damage can be identified in patients. Computerized tomography (CT scan) is used routinely in the investigation of neurological disorders, and can be used to predict possible cognitive deficits. Magnetic resonance imaging (MRI) clearly locates soft tissue changes in the brain and has become an important research tool. These imaging techniques are summarized in the Glossary.

Neuropsychological studies of patients groups with common lesion sites have resulted in the description of impairment patterns commonly occurring together, known as syndromes. For example, the dysexecutive syndrome is a collection of behavioural changes that commonly occur with damage to the anterior frontal lobe of the cerebral hemispheres, see Chapter 12.

1.1.2 Holism

The holistic view in neuropsychology proposes that mental processing occurs in parallel in subsystems or modules that are not necessarily related to anatomical areas. The disruption of the coordination of these modules may result in the emergence of the normally 'buried' lower-level activity in perception or action. This may be seen in patients as repetition of action and is known as perseveration, or the inability to initiate and terminate behaviour and action.

Returning to the analogy of the car, the control units of the engine, or their supervision by the driver, determine the performance of the engine. The function of the separate engine parts may be a secondary factor.

In the nineteenth century, the French physiologist Fluorens opposed the localization view of the phrenologists. Based on his view on animal experiments, he suggested that the cerebral cortex functions as a whole for all the mental processes of perception, cognition and intellect.

Further strong support for the unitary function of the cerebral cortex was provided by Lashley in the 1930s. In learning studies in rats he showed that functional deficits were related to the total size of damaged cortex, and not to the location of the damage.

Recently, the methods of cognitive neuropsychology have been used to identify modules in mental processing in the assessment of single patients with cerebral damage. If one aspect of performance is impaired in a patient, while others are preserved, this suggests the presence of a separate module of processing. This approach to the investigation of cognitive systems has produced assessment methods for impaired function that are not linked to particular brain areas, but instead to the components of functional skills and abilities in the brain.

1.1.3 Information processing

Cognitive psychology has since the 1950s adopted an information processing approach to the study of brain function. There is no reason to assume that all the functional systems of the brain lie in discrete anatomical areas, and there is considerable evidence to support holism, particularly in higher cognitive functions. In cognitive psychology, it is assumed that as information flows through the brain, it is processed in stages. Each processing stage is drawn as a box, and arrows show the flow of information from one stage to other stages. Hence the 'boxes and arrows' approach to brain function. Each stage can be considered as a number of neurones firing together, but these may or may not be located in one particular brain area.

In each cognitive system, the stages of processing follow an overall sequence (see Fig. 1.4):

(i)   Input processing of the information entering the brain from the senses. This can be called perceptual analysis.

(ii)   Further processing for:

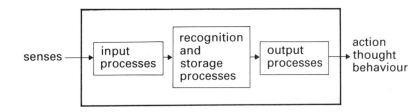

Fig. 1.4 Information processing model.

- representations or 'images' of the information for recognition. This can be called semantic analysis, or processing for meaning;
  - storage of information that can be retrieved at a later time.
(iii) output processing for transfer to action, thought or behaviour.

The information processing model in Fig. 1.4 shows the stages occurring in series from input to output. Processing stages also occur in parallel. For example, in using an object there is parallel input processing of visual, tactile and auditory information that is later combined for recognition and semantic analysis.

Cognitive neuropsychology uses an information processing approach to the study of impaired cognitive function. A patient who cannot use objects appropriately, for example cutlery in eating, or a comb and a toothbrush in dressing, may have a deficit at any one of the following stages:

- *Early visual analysis.* Can the patient match colours, shapes, or the same shapes in different size?
- *Visual representation.* Can the patient match objects, or pictures of objects?
- *Semantic system.* Can the patient match objects by function from a collection of objects or pictures of objects?
- *Action system.* Can the patient perform the movements associated with the use of an object when presented to him/her?

By assessing these stages in turn, the level of deficit may be identified, and this can be used to suggest treatment plans or compensation strategies in occupational therapy.

1.2 Overview of cerebral organization

One outcome of the studies of cerebral organization is the evidence for overall differences in the capacity to process particular information in broad areas of the cerebral cortex. The right and left cerebral hemispheres are structurally the same, but each is associated with the processing of certain types of information. Also, when the anterior

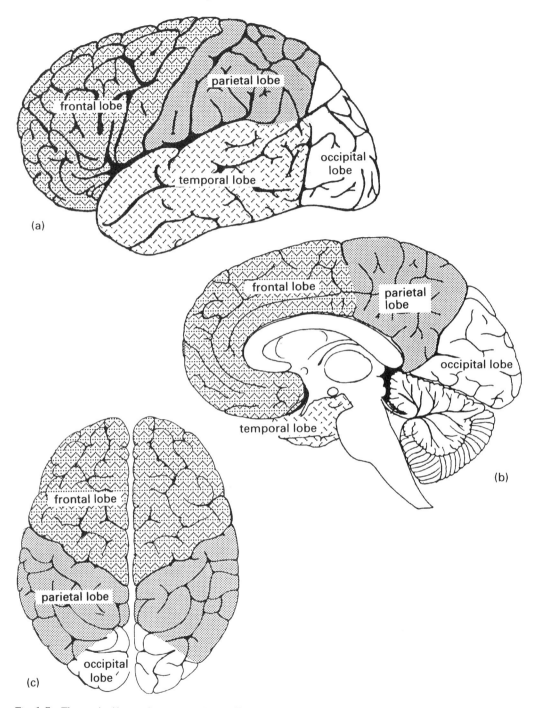

Fig. 1.5 The cerebral hemisphere seen in three different views, to identify the frontal, parietal, occipital and temporal lobes. (a) Side view of the left hemisphere. (b) Medial view of the right hemisphere seen in a sagittal section of the brain. (c) Right and left hemispheres seen from above.

and posterior divisions of the cerebral cortex are compared, some overall differences in mental processing emerge. Figure 1.5 identifies the four lobes of the cerebral hemispheres, seen in three different views, (a), (b) and (c).

1.2.1 Lateralization of function

The dominant hemisphere, usually the left, tends to be larger and heavier than the non-dominant hemisphere, (Geschwind, 1974). The inputs to the two sides from the senses, and from other brain areas and the spinal cord are largely the same, so that any difference between the two must lie in their capacity to process different types of information, see Fig. 1.6.

In most people, the *left hemisphere* is dominant for all language functions; reading, writing, the understanding and the production of speech. These functions involve the processing of sequences; letter by letter, word by word and so on. The left hemisphere is also associated

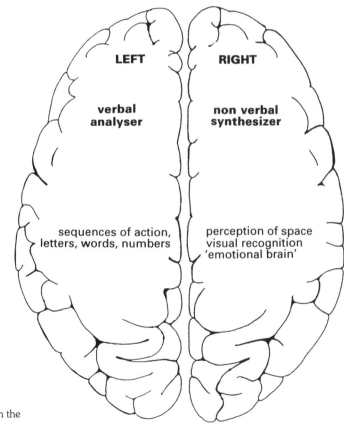

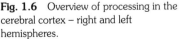

Fig. 1.6 Overview of processing in the cerebral cortex – right and left hemispheres.

with sequences of action, which are the basis of most of our movements. For example, the actions of reach, grasp, lift, lower and release are performed in series in the activity of pouring water from a jug.

All these sequential functions of language, numeracy and movement have led to the left hemisphere being called the 'analyser' (Nebes, 1974).

The *right hemisphere* has a greater capacity to process visual and spatial information that cannot be described in words. The recognition of objects, the position of body parts during movement, and the spatial relationships of objects and landmarks in extra-personal space, are associated with the right hemisphere. The right hemisphere can be called the 'synthesizer', dealing with wholes rather than parts.

Differences in affective processing in the two hemispheres have led to the right hemisphere being called the 'emotional brain'. Gainotti (1972) compared the emotional behaviour of patients with right-side lesions and those with lesions on the left. The left hemisphere patients (right hemiplegics) showed feelings of anxiety and depression, while those with right hemisphere damage (left hemiplegics) showed indifference and denial of their disabilities. Some right-side lesion patients may become depressed at a later stage in recovery, which Gainotti suggested was the result of loss of self-awareness and reduced sensitivity to others. Changes of mood, however, can have a variety of causes and they do not always reflect right hemisphere damage.

The differences in the capacity to process different types of information in the right and left hemispheres means that:

- right hemiplegic (left side lesion) patients are more likely to have language problems; and
- left hemiplegic (right side lesion) patients often have problems in visual perception.

A group study by Edmans & Lincoln (1987) showed that perceptual deficits do occur in right hemiplegia, and perceptual assessment should be included for all patients with neurological impairment.

1.2.2 Anterior/posterior organization

Some differences in overall function can also be ascribed to the posterior and anterior divisions of the cerebral cortex, separated by the central sulcus in each hemisphere, see Fig. 1.3. The parietal, occipital and temporal lobes form the posterior division. The frontal lobes form the anterior division. The anterior and posterior divisions are shown in Fig. 1.7.

The *posterior* division receives the ascending pathways from the spinal cord, and the fibre tracts from the senses project to it. Perceptual processing of these inputs occurs in the posterior cortex. The

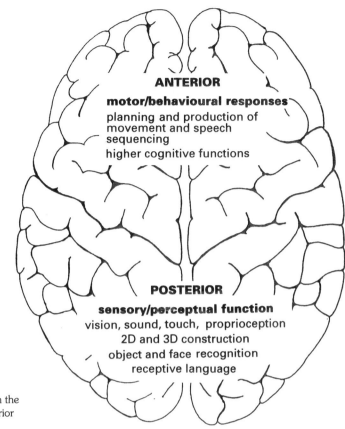

Fig. 1.7 Overview of processing in the cerebral cortex – anterior and posterior divisions.

receptive aspects of language, such as understanding written and spoken words, are also part of the posterior cortex function.

The *anterior* division receives input from the posterior cortex, and also from the lower brain centres. The output processing for the production of speech movement and behaviour occurs in the anterior cortex.

Luria (1966) was one of the first neuropsychologists to suggest that the frontal lobes integrate all components of movement and behaviour at the highest level. The anterior cortex plays an important role in higher cognitive functions such as planning, problem solving, monitoring and judgement.

These differences in processing capacity of the anterior and posterior divisions mean that:

- posterior brain damage leads to deficits in visual and spatial perception;
- anterior brain damage commonly leads to impairment of the planning and production of action and behaviour.

Memory loss is related to several brain areas and these are covered in Chapter 2, Section 2.3.

The outcome of damage in the same brain location can vary depending on the extent of cerebral damage, and on the other brain areas that may be involved. The overview of cerebral organization gives guidelines for the prediction of the possible functional problems that may result from brain damage, and for the selection of assessment procedures.

A sample of living brain tissue is neither accessible nor would it tell us very much about the complex organization of brain function. There is an ongoing exploration of mental processing in psychology based on the development of new techniques for investigation. Theories of perception and cognition are modified and extended over time.

The methods developed in neuropsychology and in cognitive neuropsychology offer guidelines for assessment and evaluation in occupational therapy by:

- the description of syndromes that are related to damage of particular brain areas, which suggest the selection of assessments in the early stages; and
- the development of appropriate assessment procedures for the individual patient, to identify which particular components of cognitive function may be impaired.

Kaplan & Hier (1982) identified a need for the adaptation of tests of perceptual and cognitive skill in order to develop realistic assessment of function in the individual patient. This relies on the therapist's understanding of the underlying cognitive systems, and his/her inventiveness.

References

Edmans, J.A. & Lincoln, N.B. (1987) The frequency of perceptual deficits after stroke. Clinical Rehabilitation, **1**, 273–81.

Gainotti, G. (1972) *Emotional behaviour and hemispheric side of lesion.* Cortex, **8**, 41–55.

Geschwind, N. (1974) The anatomical basis of hemispheric differentiation. In S.J. Dimond & J.G. Beaumont (Eds). *Hemispheric function in the human brain.* Halstead Press, New York.

Kaplan, J. & Hier, D.B. (1982) Visuospatial deficits after right hemisphere stroke. *American Journal of Occupational Therapy*, **36**, 314–21.

Luria, A.R. (1966) (B. Haigh, Transl.) *Higher cortical functions in man.* Basic Books, New York.

Nebes, R.D. (1974) Hemispheric specialization in commissurotomized man. *Psychological Bulletin*, **81**, 1–14.

Further reading

Ellis, A.W. & Young, A.W. (1988) *Human Cognitive Neuropsychology.* Chapter 1. What is cognitive neuropsychology? Lawrence Erlbaum Associates, Hove & London.

Walsh, K.W. (1987) *Neuropsychology: A clinical approach.* Churchill Livingstone, Edinburgh.

Chapter 2 Perception and Cognition in Human Occupation

From moment to moment all the senses, vision, sound, touch, pain and proprioception, pick up information from the world around us, and from inside the body. Perception is the processing in the brain that transforms all this information into our immediate experience of the world. We are usually unaware of perception, and it is very fast acting. However, perception does not only occur passively from what the brain receives via the senses. Our expectations and our past experience have an active influence on perception. Also, what we perceive may be changed by the context in which we see it.

Cognition comprises all the mental processes that allow us to recognize, to learn, to remember, and to attend to changing information in the environment. Cognition also refers to planning, problem solving, monitoring and judgement, which may be called the higher cognitive functions. Each cognitive system is a set of processing stages that operate to achieve a common goal. Several cognitive systems may be involved in one functional activity. For example, in making a phone call, finding the number, remembering it long enough to dial, and then speaking and listening, each have different cognitive demands, see Fig. 2.1.

2.1 Theories of perception

There have been two main approaches to the investigation of perception in cognitive psychology.

'Bottom-up' theories

One set of theories begin with the detailed analysis of the sensory input, and proceed to the integration of all this information with our stored knowledge of past experience. These are known as 'bottom-up' or 'data-driven' theories.

Fig. 2.1 Stages in using the telephone.

In visual perception, experiments in neurophysiology showed that the retinal image is analysed in successively more complex ways in the occipital cortex (Hubel & Wiesel, 1979). In other animal experiments, cells in the temporal cortex have been shown to respond to the presentation of faces in different views. This approach, however, does not explain how the processing output of lines and edges in the retinal image is later transformed into an object that can be recognized.

One bottom-up theory of object recognition used computer technology, which can simulate the transformation of information through successive levels of complexity (Marr, 1982). Starting with the changes in light intensity over the surface of an object, Marr showed that three successive algorithms could produce the representation of an object that can be recognized from different viewpoints. This does not mean that the brain works just like a computer, but it demonstrated the complex processing that must be involved. If perception depended only on bottom-up processing of all the incoming information from the senses, the capacity of the brain would be exceeded.

'Top-down' theories

Another set of theories of perception begin with the stored knowledge of past experience, and consider how this is used to make sense of the changing sensory input entering the brain. These are known as 'top-down' or 'concept-driven' theories. Detailed analysis of all the sensory input is not required, and this means there is economy of the processing demands. Evidence for top-down processing is found in the

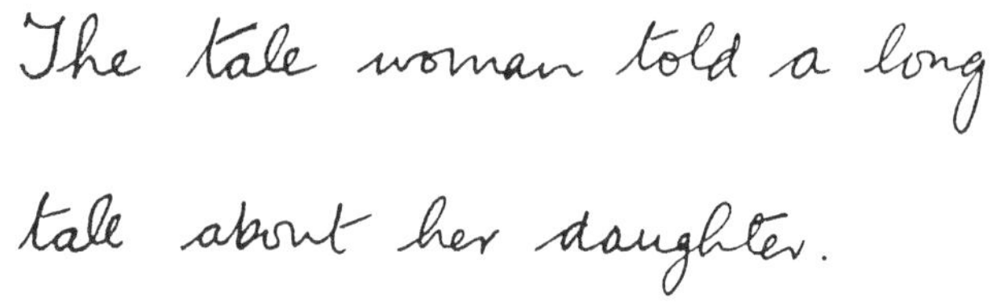

The tale woman told a long

tale about her daughter.

Fig. 2.2   Top-down processing in perception.

way we can make sense of ambiguous information. In vision, the same input to the retina can be perceived in different ways, see Fig. 2.2.

In this sentence, two of the words present the same pattern to the retina, but one is perceived as 'tall' and the other as 'tale'.

In sound, the same speech output can be perceived as different. Read aloud the following two sentences:

'That noise makes me want to scream.'
'Here is some vanilla ice cream.'

The same sensory input can only be perceived in different ways if it is influenced by our stored knowledge, and by the context in which it is presented.

It is generally agreed in psychology that perception depends on both bottom-up and top-down processing. We interpret what the senses pick up by integration with past experience. The link between perception and learned experience allows us to adapt behaviour appropriately in response to changes in the sensory input. It is important for the therapist to appreciate that perceptual deficits are not always the result of disordered sensation. The problem may originate in loss of learned adaptive responses that are linked to input from the senses.

2.2 Perception and cognition in daily living

Normal perception is so spontaneous and automatic that it is difficult to understand the experience of impaired perception in a patient with brain damage. While the effects of altered sensory input can be experienced by blindfolding our eyes or plugging our ears, understanding disordered perception is more problematic.

When the sensory input is confusing, we have to make an effort to find a solution. The responses of a group of people looking at an ambiguous figure illustrate this, see Fig. 2.3.

Some may 'see' it as an old woman, and some may 'see' it as a young woman. After a time, many will 'see' it as either one or the other, or neither and say 'I will see it when I believe it'. It is such exercises that begin to make us realize what it is like for patients with perceptual problems. For them, looking at a cup and saucer may require the same effort we needed to find a solution to the ambiguous figure.

Fig. 2.3 Ambiguous figure.

What we actually perceive at any moment depends on selective attention to the many inputs from the environment. We attend to some sensory inputs and ignore others. Also we can attend to more than one task at a time by switching from one to another. You may be able to knit and watch TV at the same time. The brain allocates attention to the various demands at any one time, but there are limits to the total processing capacity.

Finding our way around involves the processing of spatial information, to form 'spatial maps'. Negotiating a familiar route may become automatic, but if it has been changed unexpectedly, then finding the way demands attention. We can find out possessions in the familiar layout of our home or workplace, but mental effort is increased in the first few weeks when we move to a new flat or a new job.

The way we use memory depends on the cognitive demands of our own daily living. Some leisure pursuits require higher cognitive function than work tasks, and vice versa. The strategies we use to aid memory vary in different individuals. Some people use diaries and lists for memory aids, while others may rely on family and colleagues to remind them.

The performance of everyday tasks requires planning and monitoring. We need to be flexible so that the progress of the movement can be altered if the environment changes. In most activities a sequence of actions must be completed in the correct order, and we use judgement to decide when they are completed.

In cerebral damage, a component of one cognitive system may be impaired, and that component may also be part of the processing system for another ability. For example, if a patient cannot name objects, and the impairment lies in the semantic processing of the object's function, then he/she may also be unable to use objects appropriately. Brain damage also reduces the overall processing capacity of the brain, so that all activities may seem to require more mental effort. Some patients develop their own strategies to overcome their impairments. The therapist must be aware of this in the planning of assessments.

2.3 Overview of the perceptual and cognitive deficits in common neurological disorders

Experimental studies in neuropsychology over the last two decades have identified which cognitive deficits occur in particular neurological disorders, and have suggested areas for further research. Deficits in perception and cognition occur in:

- cerebral vascular accident or stroke
- traumatic head injury
- viral encephalitis
- multiple sclerosis
- Parkinson's disease
- Korsakoff's amnesia.

The cognitive changes in dementia are complicated by severe intellectual deterioration and this degenerative disorder will therefore not be included.

Brain damage resulting from a specific neurological disorder has variable effects on the function of the individual patient. The variation may be due to:

- the complex organization of the brain
- the pathology of the disease
- pre-morbid personality
- age, culture, and social background.

Some patients may have more than one neurological disorder, for example Parkinson's disease may be complicated by a stroke.

Assessment in occupational therapy is based on a problem-centred, holistic approach. The following summary gives a general guide to the cognitive deficits that are associated with the common neurological disorders treated in occupational therapy. A comprehensive account of neuropsychological studies of the degenerative diseases, including psychosocial and behavioural changes, can be found in Knight (1992).

Figure 2.4 is a view of the brain seen in sagittal section to identify the areas named in the general account of the neurological conditions below.

Cerebrovascular accident (CVA) or stroke

A stroke is a rapidly developing focal disturbance of brain function which lasts for more than 24 hours, and is vascular in origin. The impaired blood flow may be due to a haemorrhage, a thrombus or embolus, or atherosclerosis of the blood vessels. The resulting focal damage to brain tissue is called a lesion. The middle, anterior and posterior cerebral arteries are the most vulnerable to infarction. The brain areas supplied by each of these arteries is given in Appendix 1.

Various aspects of perception and cognition can be affected,

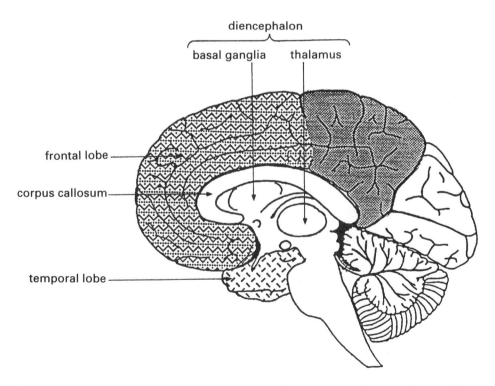

Fig. 2.4   Medial view of the right side of the brain seen in sagittal section to show the diencephalon, which is enveloped by the lobes of the cerebral hemispheres.

depending on the extent and location of the lesion, which may be on one side only, or bilateral. An overview of the deficits related to lesions in the right, left, anterior and posterior areas of the cerebral hemispheres is given in Chapter 1, Section 1.2.

Traumatic head injury

Diffuse, rather than focal, brain damage occurs in closed-head injuries. If multiple lesion sites occur, the outcome is complex and variable. Perceptual deficits may be difficult to assess due to memory problems and poor concentration. Cognitive changes are often overridden by behavioural and psychosocial problems. The impairment of memory and of higher cognitive function are common in head injuries.

Viral encephalitis

Viral encephalitis is a viral infection of the brain, which can affect many aspects of perception. A bilateral involvement of the temporal lobes results in severe memory loss characterised by rapid forgetting. The patient may not remember what happened a few moments before. Both general knowledge and skills learnt in the past are retained. Intellect is unaffected.

Multiple sclerosis

In multiple sclerosis, there is damage or loss of myelin in the central nervous system (i.e. the brain and spinal cord). Plaques form in the zones of myelin destruction, and the loss of myelin affects the rate of conduction in axons in the white matter of the brain. Lesions may occur in different places at different times. Periods of remission and exacerbation occur in the motor and sensory features of the disease, and more studies are needed to show whether cognitive changes show similar variation. It is difficult to assess cognitive abilities in multiple sclerosis if the patient has poor vision, loss of fine motor control and fatigue. Memory impairments are variable and usually mild.

A study of multiple sclerosis patients by Rao *et al.* (1989) assessed both physical and cognitive function in relation to employment potential and social functioning. Patients with cognitive dysfunction were less likely to be employed, or to engage in recreational activities, than the others, even when the level of physical disability was the same.

Parkinson's disease

Parkinson's disease is a degenerative disorder of the basal ganglia in the diencephalon of the brain. The basal ganglia link with the cerebral cortex, and particularly with the frontal lobe.

Two main areas of cognitive deficit have been described in Parkinson's disease (Brown & Marsden, 1990). One area is in the initiation and execution of a motor plan for certain actions. This has confirmed a role for the basal ganglia, together with frontal cortical areas in the planning of action. The other area is a reduction in attention capacity shown by difficulty in performing voluntary actions using both hands together. Patients with Parkinson's disease have difficulty in coordinating the motor and the perceptual aspects of movement, particularly when environmental cues are absent.

Korsakoff's amnesia

Korsakoff's amnesia results from chronic alcohol abuse. Damage to the diencephalon has been identified in this condition. Its chief feature is the inability to learn new material. The names of people met since the onset of the disease cannot be remembered. There is also loss of autobiographical memory. Skills learnt before the onset are not lost, and some studies have shown that new motor skills can be learnt.

The Korsakoff patient usually does not admit to poor memory and is unaware of the problems. Lack of awareness is the chief barrier to rehabilitation.

Many of the research studies in neuropsychology have investigated perception and cognition in stroke patients, where the deficits are more circumscribed, due to the focal nature of the lesion. Over the last decade there have been an increasing number of studies of the effects of severe head injury, and new assessment approaches are being developed. A significant trend in recent years has been the move towards assessments that are functionally based, and are made in the home environment. The value of self-assessment by the patient, and of reports from his or her carers, has also been identified.

The areas of perception and cognition that relate in particular to occupational therapy will be considered in Parts II and III under these headings:

- visual perception, object and face recognition
- spatial abilities
- action, planning and sequencing
- attention
- memory.

References

Brown, R.G. & Marsden, C.D. (1990) Cognitive function in Parkinson's disease. *Trends in neurosciences*, **13**, 21–9.

Hubel, D.H. & Wiesel, T.N. (1979) Brain mechanisms and vision. *Scientific American*, **241**, 130–44.

Knight, R.G. (1992) *The neuropsychology of degenerative brain diseases.* Lawrence Erlbaum, New Jersey.

Marr, D. (1982) *Vision. A computational investigation into the human representation and processing of visual information.* W.H. Freeman, San Francisco.

Rao, S.M., Leo, G.J., Bernadin, L. & Ellington, L. (1989) Impact of cognitive dysfunction on employment and social functioning in MS patients. *Neurology*, **39**, 143.

Further reading

Greene, J. & Hicks, C. (1984) *Basic cognitive processes.* Open University Press, Milton Keynes.

Part II   Perceptual and Cognitive Abilities

Chapter 3   Visual Perception, Object and Face Recognition

Visual perception gives meaning to all the information entering the eyes. Our perception of the visual world goes way beyond the response of light receptors in the retina of the eye, and beyond the activity of the neurones in the primary visual cortex. A larger area of the cerebral cortex is involved in the processing of vision than any of the other senses, and vision plays a major role in the total perception of the environment.

The adaptability of visual perception has been dramatically illustrated in an experiment in which subjects wore spectacles with inverting lenses. After several days, the subjects had adapted to the

Fig. 3.1 Painting a scene.

upside-down view of the world. They were able to move around normally, and perform all activities of daily living. The ability to instantly recognize the features of the visual environment seems to be so effortless that it can be difficult to appreciate how many complex processes it involves. As we look out of the window we can decide where a house ends and a tree begins if they are overlapping. Drawing or painting a scene makes us aware of clues about depth and distance, see Fig. 3.1.

Looking around a room, each object is isolated from its background, and from other objects around it. The same object is recognized irrespective of the angle we are looking at it or its distance from us. In using objects, visual recognition is associated with their meaning and their function when we use them. In social interaction we need to recognize faces and associate them with the names of the people we know. As we move about, landmarks are recognized and obstructions are avoided. Complex perceptual and cognitive processing is involved in all of these situations.

So what features of the retinal image are processed by the brain, and how are these features transformed into our perception of the three-dimensional world? The impressionist painters were able to create three-dimensional scenes from flat planes of colour on a canvas. Many different approaches have been used in psychology to study how the brain analyses the retinal image, and to describe the processes that lead to the recognition of objects.

3.1 Basic visual perception

In 1900, Lissauer was the first to introduce the term apperceptive agnosia to describe the difficulty in object recognition associated with right hemisphere lesion. This description was readdressed more recently in studies by Warrington & Taylor (1978) and Warrington (1982), who compared right and left-hemisphere lesion patients in tests of visual perception and object recognition. Warrington proposed two stages in object recognition, after early visual analysis in both occipital lobes. The right hemisphere plays a dominant role in the first stage for the perceptual categorization of objects, see Fig. 3.2.

The basic features of colour, depth, figure ground and form constancy all contribute to the perceptual analysis of an object, and each of these will now be considered.

3.1.1 Colour

Colour in the visual environment gives added meaning. As children we learn to associate the colour and the form of particular items and objects. Even in different lighting conditions, familiar objects do not

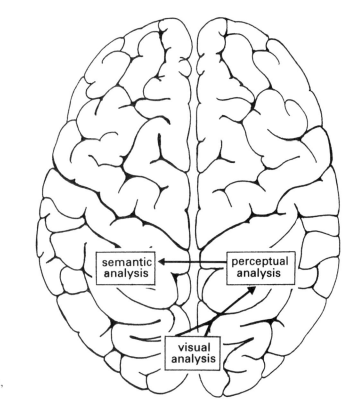

Fig. 3.2 Two stages in object recognition (adapted from Warrington, 1978).

change their colour. Similar items that may be of different colours, for example coins, or food in jars, depend on colour discrimination for identification.

Colour perception is different from colour blindness, which is a retinal defect. When there is loss of colour perception, the world is seen as shades of grey, and vision is reported as 'not clear' even though visual acuity is normal.

Selective impairment of colour and shape has been described in patients with cerebral damage. This suggests that in early visual processing, colour is processed separately from shape and depth.

3.1.2 Depth

Depth perception comes partly from the differences in the images of an object received by the retina of each eye. There are, however, other clues in the visual field which provide information about depth. If one object partly obscures another, the complete object is perceived to be nearer. When similar objects appear to be of different sizes, the larger ones are perceived to be nearer, and the smaller ones further away. Parallel lines appear to converge and textures become finer in the

Fig. 3.3 Clues for depth perception.

distance. The mugs on a tray in Fig. 3.3 illustrate these clues to depth perception.

Movement can also act as a depth cue. Sitting in a moving car, nearby features of the visual scene, such as telegraph poles, appear to move by quickly, while distant trees appear to move slowly. The perception of depth is also basic to spatial abilities, discussed in Chapter 4.

3.1.3 Figure ground

The Gestalt psychologists in the 1920s first proposed that perception is organized to produce 'good form'. They introduced the term 'figure ground'. In the visual world we perceive whole objects set in a background. All the items and objects we use must be isolated from the surfaces on which they lie and from other objects that overlap them. The three mugs shown in Fig. 3.3 form the 'figure', and the tray is the 'ground'.

Activity

Look around the room you are in and count the number of objects you can see. Then count how many of the objects are overlapped by other objects. Move to the other side of the room where you see different views of the same objects and at different distances. Note the shadows cast by the light from the window or lamp falling on the objects, and how the textures of surfaces change in the distance.

Visual perception segments the environment into what is figure and what is ground. It is the grouping together of the elements of colour, form and depth that produces the figure and separates it from the ground. Many visual illusions are pictures where figure and ground can be exchanged. Figure 3.4 can be perceived as a vase or two faces in silhouette, depending on whether the black or the white area respectively is seen as the ground.

Fig. 3.4 Figure ground – two different interpretations.

A patient with impairment of figure ground perception has difficulty in picking out objects when they are surrounded by others, for example cutlery in a drawer, or an item of clothing lying on a bed.

3.1.4 Form constancy

Objects may be seen as the same size, shape and location, even though there are variations in their image on the retina. This is known as perceptual constancy, and without it the visual world would be very confusing.

The table on which I write appears the same size when I stand one metre away from it or six metres across the room. As I move about the room, I do not see the table moving about even though the image of the table on my retina is changing. If I tilt my head to one side the retinal image again changes but the table appears the same.

Object constancy also allows us to identify the same object when it is seen in different views and orientations, see Fig. 3.5. If we are shown an unfamiliar object, we can still identify it as the same object when we see it from above, from below, at an angle, and so on. This is known as perceptual categorization, which is different from the recognition of a known object

Size discrimination is also part of form constancy perception. We can distinguish the same shape seen in different sizes from other shapes or objects.

In summary, the perception of colour, shape, figure ground and form constancy combine to complete the perceptual processing that leads to the representation of an object in all views. In right hemisphere lesion (left hemiplegia), object recognition dysfunction originates in the ability to complete this visual perceptual analysis of objects.

Fig. 3.5 Object constancy – object seen in different orientations.

Patients with left hemisphere lesion (right hemiplegia), however, have intact perceptual processing, but it cannot be integrated with stored knowledge about object meaning and function. Lissauer called this associative agnosia, or impairment of the semantic analysis, shown in Fig. 3.2. Patients with visual semantic deficits may show good recognition of single objects, but poor functional use of objects.

3.2 Visual object recognition

The ability to use objects depends on the integration of visual perceptual processing with the knowledge of object function. The ecological approach to visual perception (Neisser, 1976; Gibson, 1979) emphasizes how the textures, surfaces and lines in the visual environment give meaning to what we see, and how these are interpreted in the context of the changing scene around us. Most objects have a function, and their visual structure is related to it. Gibson suggested that objects 'afford' function, for example the visual perceptual input from a brush is integrated with the actions for cleaning a surface, (see Chapter 5, Fig. 5.6).

Objects in the real world are seen in context. Palmer (1975) explored the effect of context on the ability to recognize objects. Normal subjects were presented with a scene, followed by a very brief glimpse of the picture of an object. In some cases the object was appropriate to the scene, and in other cases it was not. Recognition of the object was significantly better when the object was appropriate to the contextual scene. It was also better than when no scene was presented before the object.

The importance of contextual information in visual object recognition supports the inclusion of the functional assessment of patients being carried out in a familiar environment with objects previously known to them.

In occupational therapy it is important to appreciate that problems in the use of objects can arise for a variety of reasons (Toglia, 1989). Assessment aimed at identifying the nature of the deficit as precisely as possible can also be used to suggest the types of cueing that may be beneficial, and to identify the particular areas of task performance where problems may arise. Toglia suggests that assessment in occupational therapy should also be extended to include the effects of the number of objects present, the spatial arrangement of the objects, the complexity of the task, and the environment.

Single case-studies of patients with poor object recognition have shown that impairment can occur at several levels of processing. An information processing model of object recognition (Ellis & Young, 1988) that has been developed from the results of these single case-studies is shown in Fig. 3.6.

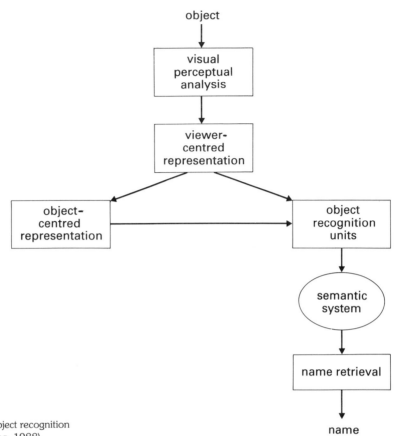

Fig. 3.6 Model of object recognition
(based on Ellis & Young, 1988).

The viewer-centred representation is the level of processing that describes an object from the viewpoint of the observer. This level is intact if the patient can copy line drawings and match objects.

The object-centred representation is the basis of object constancy, which leads to recognition of an object when presented in any view. This level can be assessed by matching and recognition of the same object in different views.

The object recognition units are stored descriptions of known objects. The outputs from the viewer-centred and the object-centred representations are compared with these stored descriptions for recognition of a known object. The object recognition units form the link between the visual and the semantic systems.

In the semantic system the output from visual recognition processing accesses stored knowledge of the meaning and function of objects. The semantic representation may also be accessed from tactile input, or from a verbal description of an object. If there is no deficit in the semantic system, objects can be matched by function and can be used appropriately. Impairment at this level has been called semantic agnosia (Humphreys & Riddoch, 1987).

For the naming of objects, output from the semantic system must access the lexicon of names of known objects. Output from the semantic system must also access the action system to activate the movements that are associated with the use of the object.

This model of object recognition extends the description of the two stages first outlined by Lissauer to several levels, which can be identified by tests of matching in same or different views, and matching by function, see Chapter 9.

Accounts of current theories of visual object recognition, and of the single case-studies that led to the development of the model, are given in the further reading at the end of the chapter.

3.3 Face recognition

The recognition of faces is not the same as recognition of objects; a face offers so much more information than an object. In a face we are presented with expressions of emotion, and with speech, both of which are unique to that person. We link this information with a person's age, sex, occupation and behaviour, and these influence the way we interact with people. In common with objects, a face can be processed as a visual structure, recognized as a face when seen from different views, and we know whether a face is familiar or not. The identity of a known person, however, can be recognized just from the sound of his or her voice, or from a fleeting glimpse in a crowd.

The model of face processing described by Bruce & Young (1986) is based on single case-studies of patients with problems in recognizing familiar faces, see Fig. 3.7. This model illustrates the complexity of the system involved.

The first stage is a visual perceptual analysis of a face, which distinguishes the visual elements of that face; the eyes, the nose, the mouth, and so on. A patient who has a disruption at this early stage is unable to distinguish these basic features of a face, and he or she is likely to have more widespread perceptual difficulties.

The next stage of the model shows parallel processing of several different types of information associated with faces:

- analysis of facial expressions based on movements of the muscles of the face;
- analysis of facial speech, based on the movements of the mouth and the tongue in speaking;
- visual description of faces, which allow us to distinguish and match faces;

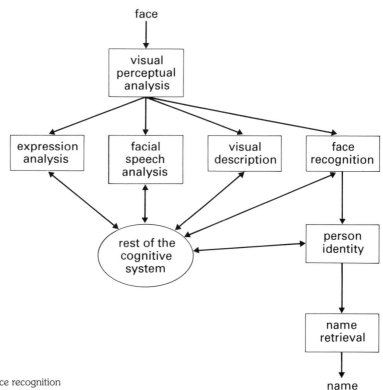

Fig. 3.7 Model of face recognition
(based on Bruce & Young, 1986).

- face recognition of known faces, but not at the level of identification of a particular person.

Face recognition at this level is based on the ability to discriminate the faces of unfamiliar people, and to match different views of an unfamiliar face.

The output from all these parallel stages leads to the stage of recognition of the identity of a particular known person. Bruce and Young suggest that access to this final recognition stage is also reached via other semantic knowledge about known people, such as family relationships or occupation. Bruce & Young call this 'the rest of the cognitive system'.

The final stage of processing in the model concerns access to the stored names of people we know, and retrieval of a particular name.

In occupational therapy patients present with a variety of problems associated with poor recognition of faces. Poor face recognition is most often found in the stroke patient with bilateral lesions, or the head-injured patient with multiple posterior lesions. Advice to relatives and friends on the importance of the voice and facial expressions can reduce the stress for the patient. If the problem also includes an inability to learn the names of the hospital staff, the origin may be a loss of memory, and this needs to be assessed by differential diagnosis.

Summary

(1) Visual perception organizes the visual environment into a meaningful whole. Perception includes the isolation of shapes and objects from their background, and the ability to recognize them in a variety of viewing conditions. These two features are known as figure ground and form constancy respectively.
(2) Some theories of visual perception have considered bottom-up processing, from the analysis of the retinal image to more complex recognition processing. Other top-down processing theories emphasize the importance of the past experience to make sense of sensory input information in terms of expectations about the visual world.
(3) Object recognition depends on:
    (a) the complete visual perceptual analysis of the object;
    (b) recognition processing to the level of a representation that is independent of viewpoint;
    (c) processing for meaning in the semantic system.
    Impairment at the semantic level leads to poor functional use of objects.
    The recognition of faces involves additional processing of facial speech and facial expressions.
(4) Visual perceptual processing has been linked to the right hemisphere, and semantic processing to the left hemisphere in studies of patients with problems in object recognition. Severe impairment of the recognition of objects and faces may only occur in bilateral lesions, or the problem may originate in memory.

References

Bruce, V. & Young, A. (1986) Understanding face recognition. *British Journal of Psychology*, **77**, 305–27.
Ellis, A.W. & Young, A.W. (1988) *Human cognitive neuropsychology.* Lawrence Erlbaum, London.
Gibson, J.J. (1979) *The ecological approach to visual perception.* Houghton Mifflin, Boston.
Humphreys, G.W. & Riddoch, M.J. (1987) *To see or not to see. A case study of visual agnosia.* Lawrence Erlbaum, London.
Neisser, U. (1976) *Cognition and reality.* W.H. Freeman, San Francisco.
Palmer, S.E. (1975) The effect of contextual scenes on the identification of objects. *Memory & Cognition*, **3**, 519–26.

Toglia, J.P. (1989) Visual perception of objects. An approach to assessment and intervention. *American Journal of Occupational Therapy*, **43**, 587–95.

Warrington, E.K. (1982) Neuropsychological studies of object recognition. *Philosophical Transactions of the Royal Society* (London), **B 298**, 15–33.

Warrington, E.K. & Taylor, A.M. (1978) Two categorical stages in object recognition. *Perception*, **7**, 695–705.

Further reading

Ellis, A.W. & Young, A.w. (1988) *Human cognitive neuropsychology.* Lawrence Erlbaum Associates, London and Hove.
  Chapters 2 and 4. Details of single case studies of patients with problems in object and face recognition.

Eysenck, M.W. & Keane, M.T. (1990) *Cognitive Psychology. A student's handbook.* Lawrence Erlbaum Associates, London & Hove.
  Chapters 2 and 3. Theoretical approaches to visual perception, object and face recognition.

Govier, H. & Govier, E. (1991) Basic perceptual processes. In J. Radford & E. Govier, (Eds) *A textbook of psychology.* Routledge, London.
  Chapter 10. A clear account of the perception of objects, depth perception, and bottom up and top down processing.

Chapter 4 Spatial Abilities

In the exploration of near space we scan the area of space offered by the visual field ahead, and beyond by moving the eyes and the head. Once an object or a surface has been located, spatial perception then analyses its relation to other objects around, and to ourselves. In

Fig. 4.1 Map of a maze.

movement, the spatial relations of the moving body parts are integrated with the spatial perception of the space that is used. Spatial perception is crucial in drawing, and in assembling the parts of the equipment we use at work and in daily living.

On a larger scale, the spatial relations of buildings and landmarks are important in finding our way around on foot, on a bicycle or in a car. We need to discriminate right and left, and to be able to mentally rotate a pathway to follow it in different directions, see Fig. 4.1.

Building up a mental spatial map of familiar surroundings may change the task of route finding into one of spatial memory. In this chapter the exploration of near and far space will be considered.

4.1 Scanning of space

The area of the visual field ahead determines the space that is available for visual and spatial perception without moving the eyes. The visual field is like a window to the visual world. The view through this window can be scanned by movements of the eyes. Movements of the head take the window to different positions around the scene ahead, and this increases the area that can be scanned.

4.1.1 Visual field

If we look straight ahead the area of the visual world that is visible out of each eye is known as the visual field for that eye. The right and left visual fields overlap in the midline, so that some light from each visual field reaches the retina of both eyes.

'Blind areas' may appear in the visual fields as a result of disruption at any level in the visual pathway from the retina to the occipital cortex itself. The opportunity for visuospatial perception without head movement is then restricted.

The visual pathway from one visual field reaches the occipital lobe of the opposite side, as in Fig. 4.2. Follow the projection from the left visual field to the inner nasal half of the left retina, and to the outer temporal half of the right retina. Now continue the same path (shown in black) on to the optic chiasma, and then to the right occipital lobe. You should now appreciate how damage to one occipital lobe can produce 'blind areas' in half the visual field of each eye.

Patients with posterior cerebral lesions due to a vascular accident, or with head injury, may have 'blind areas' of varying size and position in the visual fields, depending on the particular level of disruption of the visual pathway. These patients usually compensate successfully for this defect by movements of the head.

An estimate of the area of the normal visual field can be shown in the following way:

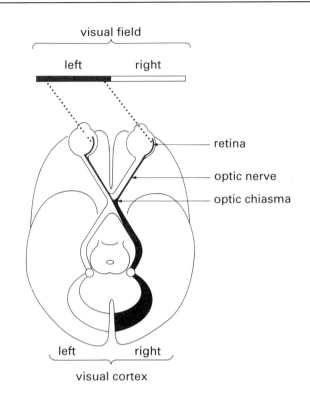

Fig. 4.2 Visual field and the visual pathway. Information from the left visual field enters both eyes, and reaches the right visual cortex. In the same way, the right visual field projects to the left visual cortex.

Activity

Stand behind a partner and ask him/her to focus on an object straight ahead. Place your fingers at different positions to the right, left, above and below, and ask your partner to report when the fingers are seen.

Experience of how loss of part of the visual fields affects perception can be gained by the following:

Activity

Cut out quarters or halves of a circle in black paper. Stick pairs of corresponding shapes on to the inner half of one lens and the outer half of the other lens of a pair of spectacles. Wear these spectacles while you walk about, write, read and make a cup of coffee.

4.1.2 Eye movements

Most of the time we scan the space around us by moving the eyes and the head. The movements of the eyes are controlled by the brain stem and part of the frontal lobe.

In scanning a static display, such as the page of a book, the eyes move in a particular way. Quick movements, known as saccades, alternate with stationary periods of fixation. The points of fixation allow light from a word, or a group of words, to be focused on the central area of the retina.

Saccadic eye movements can be seen in the following way:

Activity

Ask a partner to move his/her eyes in a straight line from left to right. Again you will see the eyes make saccades and fixations.

In scanning a larger area such as a picture, the eyes first make long saccades from the centre to the periphery, followed by shorter and shorter saccades to fixate on the detail of the picture.

A different type of eye movement occurs when the eyes follow a moving target.

Activity

Ask a partner to fixate on the tip of a pencil which you move across from left to right. Observe how the eyes move smoothly as they follow the target.

This smooth eye movement is called pursuit movement, and its central control is separate from that for saccadic movements. Normal pursuit eye movements are essential for many sports activities. The eyes must follow a ball as it moves towards a bat or a racquet. The head-injured person may be able to throw a ball by focusing on the target ahead, but he/she cannot catch the ball if the eyes cannot follow the flight back again.

Awareness of the space around us also involves shifts of attention without eye movements. In the same way that we orient to one noise and then another without moving the head, we are aware of changes in the visual environment without moving the head or the eyes. If we are engrossed in a task, we can be aware of someone else entering the room without moving the eyes.

Orientation to stimuli in the space around depends initially on the available area of the visual fields, the movements of the eyes, and on shifts of attention which may or may not involve eye movements.

4.2 Spatial perception

A wide range of abilities contribute to the perception of near space, which includes personal and reaching space, see Fig. 4.3.

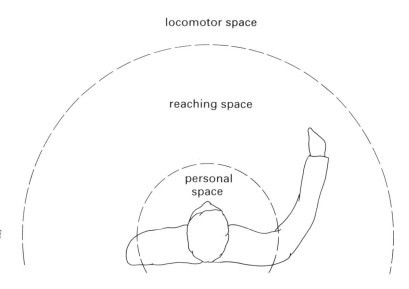

locomotor space

reaching space

personal space

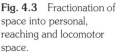

Fig. 4.3 Fractionation of space into personal, reaching and locomotor space.

The visual perceptual system processes the features of form, depth and figure ground, and also the detail of the textures of surfaces and the orientation of lines which form part of spatial perception. Further input from auditory and tactile perception give clues about the position of many features of the environment. When there is a deficit in one of the components of spatial perception, then more reliance is placed on the other components. For example, a patient with a severe spatial deficit may negotiate stairs by crawling up them, if he or she can no longer rely on visual perception of the depth of the steps.

4.2.1 Constructional ability

All activities in personal and reaching space are carried out within the spatial framework between ourselves and the objects we manipulate. In any construction task, single units are assembled into a two or three-dimensional whole. In drawing, the parts must be placed in the correct relative positions to the whole, in two dimensions on the page. Many domestic and work activities include fitting together the component parts of equipment in a particular three-dimensional arrangement. There is a large spatial component to maintenance and repair tasks, such as fixing a car engine or a lawn mower, see Fig. 4.4.

The mental representation of spatial processing has not been investigated in the same detail as visual perception, because of the difficulty in isolating the spatial component from other perceptual processing. Many studies in neuropsychology have analysed the drawings and the constructional abilities of patients with right or left-hemisphere lesion by asking them to copy drawings, and to assemble coloured blocks into a given design. Failure in these tasks could be the

Fig. 4.4 Constructional ability.

result of deficits in the output to the action system, rather than in spatial processing. Detailed scrutiny of the types of errors has distinguished poor spatial organization from an inability to organize the movements involved.

In a task of copying two dimensional drawings, Warrington *et al.* (1966) found a difference in the type of errors shown by right and left hemisphere lesion patients. The drawings made by the right hemisphere patients showed disruption of the spatial arrangement of the parts, while the left hemisphere lesion patients produced simplified drawings, which could be accounted for by poor execution of the movements required.

4.2.2 Body scheme

The perception of the relative position of the body parts of space is known as body scheme. In all movement, the spatial relationship between the different body parts is constantly changing. Sensory input from the proprioceptors in the muscles and the joints provides information about the position of the body parts at any moment. This proprioceptive input from each part is integrated into the spatial perception of all the parts in body scheme. Patients with body scheme disorder have difficulties with constructional tasks and often appear to be clumsy. They cannot link the location of points in the environment with the extent and direction of movement, even though proprioception may be normal.

The motor output in construction ability requires the planning and organizing of movements in relation to spatial elements of a task. When objects are moved by the hand the output of the spatial processing is integrated into the motor system for correct programming of the muscle action. When the deficit is in the action system it is known as constructional apraxia, see Chapter 11.

Studies of body scheme disorder in relation to locus of lesion have proved inconclusive when the assessment relies on verbal responses by the patient.

In a study of dressing performance in adult patients with CVA by Warren (1981), body scheme was assessed with body identification (using finger identification, body parts and right/left discrimination), and body revisualization (using construction of a body puzzle, and a draw-a-person test). Patients with severe aphasia were eliminated from the study, but 30% of the remaining left-hemisphere lesion patients were unable to complete the test because of language problems.

In a study by Semmes *et al.* (1963), patients were given a diagram of the body with the parts identified by numbers, and they were asked to touch the corresponding parts of their own bodies. It was found that patients with left parietal lesions were more impaired than right-side lesion patients in the discrimination of body parts.

Spatial knowledge is important for all activities in personal and reaching space, particularly when there is a constructional element to the task. The spatial orientation of the parts of the body to each other is basic to all the movements associated with these tasks. The complex nature of spatial perception, however, means that a wide range of discrete abilities are involved in all exploration of space (De Renzi, 1982).

4.3 Route finding

Large-scale spatial knowledge is part of finding the way round our surroundings. This area of space can be called locomotor space to distinguish it from near space, as in Fig. 4.3.

You can begin to appreciate the features of route finding by remembering an experience of moving to a new home, or arriving at college or a new place of work. You probably chose different strategies in starting to find your way around. Asking someone the way provided information about landmarks – 'go along here until you reach the library . . .'; and about directions – 'right or left'. You could use this verbal information to trace the route mentally. If there were few people around, a map of the new district or the campus or the hospital, gave visual information about routes. Mental rotation of the visual map was probably needed to transfer the map into the route you needed. After a time, it was necessary to find the way between two points by different routes. One route was better than another when it was raining, or if you needed wheelchair access for a patient. The route between two

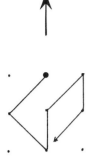

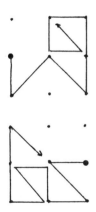

Fig. 4.5 A nine-dot test for route finding. Examples of the visual maps. (Semmes *et al. Journal of Psychology,* **39**, 227–44, 1955.

locations could also be constructed from the combination of the mental image of two known routes.

With practice the spatial layout of new surroundings is learnt and moving around becomes automatic. Some people say that they have no sense of direction and others say that they cannot read maps. This highlights the individual differences in the strategies that are used and in the various cognitive functions that are involved in the exploration of locomotor space. The opportunity to demonstrate this arises with first-year students in their first weeks on campus, or with therapists at a meeting or study day held at a hospital unknown to the participants.

Activity

Form three groups of subjects. Each group is given the same task of finding the way to an unknown location, and returning to the start.

Group 1 is given a simple map of the route.
Group 2 is given verbal instructions of how to get there.
Group 3 is led through the route, on the outward journey only, by someone who knows the building.

Note which group returns first (and who does not return!). How important was information about landmarks on the way? Compare the experiences of each group.

Studies in cognitive psychology have suggested that large-scale spatial knowledge may be acquired in the form of a mental map (Pick & Lockman, 1981), but this does not explain how the information is stored, or how it is used. Errors made in route finding are not the same as losing a piece of a map. The brain does not have the capacity to store maps of all our familiar surroundings, and little is known about how spatial knowledge is organized in memory. One of the possible ways that spatial knowledge is retrieved and used in short-term memory is described in the working memory model in Chapter 7.

Studies in neuropsychology of patients with problems in route finding have related the ability to follow maps with the locus of brain lesion. Semmes *et al.* (1955) studied 76 war veterans in USA who had localized gunshot wounds in the brain. Nine discs were placed on the floor in three rows of three, and north was marked on the wall. The patients were given cards with the same arrangement of dots, and a route traced between them, either with a line (visual modality), or with tacks and a cord between (tactile modality), see Fig. 4.5. The patients were asked to walk round the route indicated on each card. The patients with right or left parietal lobe lesions showed significantly poorer performance than the other patients and the normal controls. There was no difference in performance with the visual and tactile maps.

A later study of war veterans by Ratcliffe & Newcombe (1973) compared anterior and posterior lesion patients, and found impairment in the bilateral posterior lesion group. The better performance by those with unilateral lesions may have been due to the development of compensation strategies.

Route finding involves direction sense, right/left discrimination, the identification of landmarks, and the ability to orient the body to the spatial layout of the environment. Following a route in familiar surroundings becomes a memory task. Both normal and brain damaged people seem to use various strategies. Some may rely on visuospatial cues, while others may verbally code the path to be followed. It follows that the rehabilitation of patients with route finding problems relies on reinforcing previous strategies, or developing new ones.

Summary

(1) Orientation to the features of the space around demands:
    ● an adequate area of intact visual fields
    ● scanning movements of the eyes
    ● shifts of attention without eye movements.
(2) Spatial perception in reaching space locates single objects or surfaces with respect to other objects, and in relation to ourselves.
(3) The spatial relations of the body parts in body scheme is integrated into spatial perception when the upper limbs manipulate objects, and when the lower limbs negotiate steps or kerbs.
(4) Studies of normal subjects suggest that the mental representation of far space has many of the characteristics of a 'cognitive map'. In finding the way in the large-scale spatial environment, the recognition of landmarks, direction sense, and body orientation, are all part of the spatial processing involved.
(5) The inability to form a mental representation of space may be a factor in the phenomenon of unilateral neglect. This is discussed in Chapter 6.

References

Pick, H.L. & Lockman, J.J. (1981) From frames of reference to spatial representations. In L.S. Liben, A.H. Patterson & N. Newcombe. (Eds) *Spatial representation and behaviour across life span*. Academic Press, New York.

Ratcliffe, G. & Newcombe, F. (1973) Spatial orientation in man: effects of left, right and bilateral cerebral lesions. *Journal of Neurological Neurosurgery & Psychiatry*, **36** 448–54.

Semmes, J., Weinstein, S., Ghent, L. & Teuber, H.L. (1955) Spatial orientation in man after cerebral injury. 1. Analysis by locus of lesion. *Journal of Psychology*, **39** 227–44.

Semmes, J., Weinstein, S., Ghent, L. & Teuber, H.L. (1963) Correlates of impaired orientation in personal and extrapersonal space. *Brain*, **86** 747–72.

Warren, M. (1981) Relationship of constructional apraxia and body scheme disorders to dressing performance in adult CVA. *American Journal of Occupational Therapy*, **35** 431–7.

Warrington, E.K., James, M. & Kinsbourne, M. (1966) Drawing disability in relation to laterality of cerebral lesion. *Brain*, **89** 53–82.

Further reading

De Renzi, E. (1982) *Disorders of space exploration and cognition*. Wiley, New York.

   Chapter 7: Disorders of personal space cognition

   Chapter 8: Disorders of topographical memory.

Gianutsos, R. & Matheson, P. (1987) The rehabilitation of visual perceptual disorders attributable to brain injury. In Meier, M.J., Benton, A.L. & Diller, L. (Eds) *Neuropsychological Rehabilitation*. Churchill Livingstone, Edinburgh.

   Visual field and eye movements.

Smyth, M.M., Morris, P.E., Levy, P. & Ellis, A.W. (1987) Cognition in Action. Lawrence Erlbaum, London.

   Chapter 11: Arriving in a new city: Acquiring and using spatial knowledge.

Chapter 5   Action, Planning and Sequencing

In all our movements, the output from the brain produces changes in the pattern of activity in groups of muscles. The outcome depends on the function of a complex system of motor centres in many brain areas, and on sensory feedback from the muscles and joints. Movement problems in patients with neurological impairment are complex and varied. Those originating in the motor and/or sensory systems can be identified by the assessment of sensation, muscle tone, brain-stem and spinal reflexes. Some patients with minimal motor or sensory loss have movement problems, however, particularly in relation to the use of objects.

In task performance, actions are planned in advance and the action

Fig. 5.1   Mismatch of object and action in a sequence with multiple objects.

plans must be integrated with knowledge of the objects and their function. When more than one object is used, there must be correct matching between the object and the action at each stage. In impaired cognitive function there may be mismatch of object and action, as in Fig. 5.1.

Actions are combined in a particular order to achieve a goal. For example, in photocopying a sheet of paper, the lid is lifted, the paper located on the glass, the lid lowered, and the start button pressed. The task can only be completed if the stages are planned and performed in the correct order or *sequence*.

Mental processing for action involves a complex system, and many questions remain unanswered. Studies of the acquisition of motor skills in normal movement have produced processing models of motor behaviour (Scott Kelso, 1982). Single case-studies of patients with cerebral damage have demonstrated the role of visual and verbal input in the performance of movement associated with objects. In many neurologically impaired patients the presence of physical motor deficits and/or language problems complicates the assessment of the initiation and the production of actions related to objects. Patients with low functional levels may present as confused or lacking in concentration. The aim of this chapter is to give some understanding of mental processing of action in relation to task performance.

5.1 Programs for action

In the 1970s, psychologists who were interested in the acquisition of motor skills developed information processing models of normal motor behaviour.

5.1.1 The motor program

The production of movement requires the activation of many groups of muscles from the motor areas of the brain. The set of motor commands for a particular movement can be called a motor program. Keele (1968) defined the motor program as an abstract memory trace that is activated before a movement begins. A motor program (also known as an engram) can be activated internally by volition, or externally by changes in the environment. The visual input from the structure of an object with a handle may activate the movement of gripping. The motor program specifies not only which muscles are active but also the direction, force and timing of the muscle activity. This can be compared with a computer program which executes a series of functions when the program is activated. In the same way that computer programs are stored as files on a floppy disc, motor programs are stored as action memory traces in the brain.

One problem with this original definition of a motor program is that it does not account for the execution of a particular movement by different groups of muscles. For example, you can write your signature using different muscle groups.

Activity

Sign your name on a small piece of paper using the fingers to move the pencil. Then sign your name on a wall mounted board using the muscles of the shoulder and the elbow. The signature is the same, even though different muscle groups have been used in each case.

The open-loop model in Fig. 5.2 shows how a movement command system generates motor programs which activate muscles via the motor cortex.

This model can account for the execution of simple ballistic movements that may be programmed before the start. If you press a computer key or a piano key, or throw a piece of paper into a waste basket, once you have started there is no chance of changing the movement.

Most of our movements take longer than this, and we do make changes in response to feedback from the muscles and any changes in the environment. As we pour water from a kettle into a cup, we modify

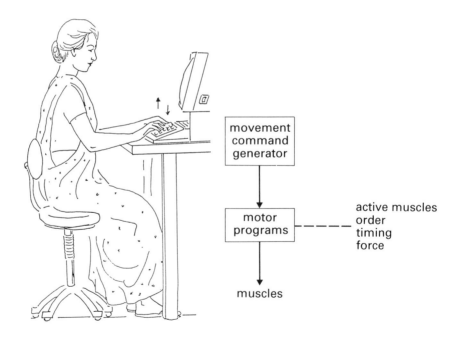

Fig. 5.2   Open loop model of ballistic movements.

the movement as it proceeds in response to the weight of the kettle, and to the level of the water in the cup.

A closed loop model developed by Adam (1971), as in Fig. 5.3, includes feedback of sensory information from the proprioceptors in the muscles of the moving limbs and from exteroceptors (visual, auditory and tactile). There are now two memory traces for each movement:

- the action memory trace that initiates the movement (motor program)
- the perceptual trace which grows as a function of feedback.

Repetition and rehearsal of a movement increase the strength of the perceptual trace. In the early stages of learning, when the perceptual trace is weak and poorly defined, intrinsic error correction is poor, and the benefits of verbal prompting and cueing are great. This is called the verbal motor stage. In the later stage of learning, the perceptual trace is strong, and resistant to forgetting. At that stage errors can be corrected by direct matching of the perceptual trace to the motor program.

The theory of motor performance, which is based on the generation of motor programs modified by comparison with perceptual input, can provide some understanding of movement problems following cerebral damage. Poor initiation of movement may be the result of the loss of stored motor programs, or of the ability to construct or modify

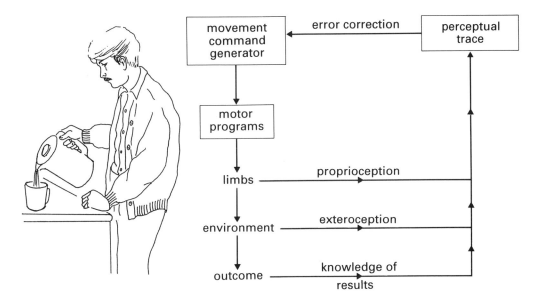

Fig. 5.3   Closed loop model with feedback during movement (Adam, 1971).

them. Perceptual problems may reduce the option of error correction during the progress of movement.

5.1.2 Movement schema

The original definition of a motor program raises the question of how we store all the motor programs for the large number of movements we make. It has been estimated that 100,000 motor programs would be needed for the production of speech movements alone.

The term 'schema' is used widely in psychology for a set of memory structures developed from past experience and used as the basis of a plan for future action. A motor scheme is a generalized motor program activated for all the movements associated with a common motor pattern (Schmidt, 1975). For example, a motor scheme for reaching and grasping is used to reach for a cup on a table, a packet of food in a cupboard, or the hand of a child. The difference between these movement patterns is the direction and extent (force) of the movement, and the constraints of the object being grasped.

Schema theory suggests that a motor scheme for a particular movement pattern grows with practice in different situations. This supports the value of variable practice in the early stages of learning. A motor scheme for reaching and grasping is strengthened by practice of all the activities that incorporate this movement pattern. The principle of training transfer, used widely in physical education programmes and in rehabilitation, is supported by schema theory.

5.2 Sequences of action

All learnt complex movements involve sequences of single actions that are linked in a particular order to complete a task or reach a goal.

Studies of errors made in performing sequences of actions suggest a hierarchy in the activation of a scheme. Reason & Mycielska (1982) asked 98 people to keep a diary of the times when their actions were not those they intended. The study collected a total of 625 errors, and these were grouped into four types:

(i)   actions repeated unnecessarily
(ii)   actions made in relation to the wrong object
(iii) intrusion of an irrelevant action in a sequence
(iv)   omission of action.

Think of examples of each of these errors that you have made. For example, sugaring your tea twice, putting coffee into the teapot, forgetting to go into gear before starting to drive. Reason & Mycielska suggested that when a high-level schema for a sequence is activated, sub-scheme are then activated in order. The sub-schema require checking and errors are more likely to occur at transition points from one sub-schema to the next. For example, getting into gear is a transition point between switching on the ignition and pressing the accelerator in the scheme for starting to drive.

It was noted in the study that many of the errors occurred in familiar environments, and when the subject was planning other activities at the same time. You may have omitted the action of 'lock the door' in the sequence for leaving the house when you have an important case presentation that day.

Studies of patients with left hemisphere lesions have shown that similar action errors are made by patients in task performance. The most common error made by patients, however, is perseveration of action in a sequence. The same action is repeated several times and there is an inability to move on to the next action in the sequence.

Lehmkuhl & Poeck (1981) compared the performance of brain damaged patients in tests involving arranging pictures in the correct order both when the pictures related to a story and when they illustrated action sequences. These action sequences included between five and seven photographs of actions such as: brushing teeth; opening a tin and pouring the contents into a pan; telephoning; and punching paper and putting it into a file. The apraxic patients in the group performed significantly worse than the others in sequencing the pictures of the stages of everyday action. This study suggests that knowledge of action sequencing and of common events can be selectively impaired.

5.3 Initiation and production of action

There are several ways in which actions can be generated. Movement can be initiated by verbal, visual or tactile input, or by volition. The verbal input to movement is by command. We are able to respond to the command 'Show me how you would use a comb' by demonstrating the actions of combing the hair. When the actions are self-initiated, they are generated internally and may also be mediated through language. When the object is present, both vision and touch provide perceptual input to initiate the actions. It is difficult to separate these components in patients who have both motor and language problems.

The terms apraxia and dyspraxia are used to describe difficulty in performing skilled movements to reach a goal. In this section we will consider some of the studies carried out in neuropsychology to investigate the cognitive system in relation to purposeful movement. A description of the different types of apraxia is found in Chapter 11.

5.3.1 The neuroanatomical model

In 1900, Liepman was the first to describe a movement disorder in patients who were unable to make purposeful movements, even though they had no muscle weakness or sensory loss. Liepman described a neuroanatomical model of apraxia based on studies of patients with left-hemisphere lesion, see Fig. 5.4.

In learned skilled movement, actions are activated from an action memory store in the left parietal lobe. This area projects to the left frontal motor areas for the production of movement of the right side of the body. For skilled movements of the left side of the body, impulses must cross to the motor areas of the right frontal lobe via the corpus callosum. More recent studies by Geschwind (1975) have supported this model.

A group study (Heilman *et al.*, 1975) found that apraxic patients showed poor performance in learning and retaining motor skills, compared with other non-apraxic left-hemisphere lesion patients.

The motor areas in the frontal lobe include the primary motor cortex that projects directly to the muscles via the corticospinal pathway. Two other motor areas lie anterior to the primary motor cortex:

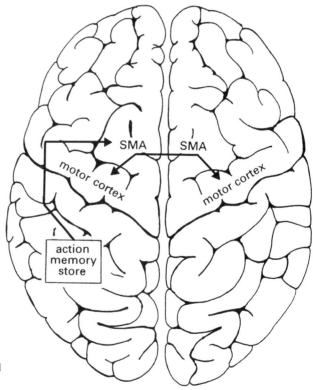

Fig. 5.4 Liepman's neuroanatomical model of apraxia (SMA=supplemental motor area).

- The supplemental motor area (SMA), which lies on the medial aspect of the frontal lobe. The SMA is active before a movement begins.
- The pre-motor cortex, which lies anterior to the primary area. The pre-motor cortex responds to the output from visual perceptual processing.

These two areas (the SMA and pre-motor cortex) cooperate in the activation of the primary motor area in the planning and performance of skilled movement (Goldberg, 1985).

5.3.2 The information processing model

Studies in cognitive neuropsychology have focused on the activation of motor programs for action from verbal and from visual perceptual routes. To date there have been few studies of the role of tactile input.

A patient with dyspraxia in the use of objects may have impairment of object recognition, see chapter 3, figure 3.6. Three other possible levels of impairment will now be considered based on the model shown in figure 5.5. These are firstly, the semantic system for action; secondly, the direct route from vision; and thirdly, the verbal route.

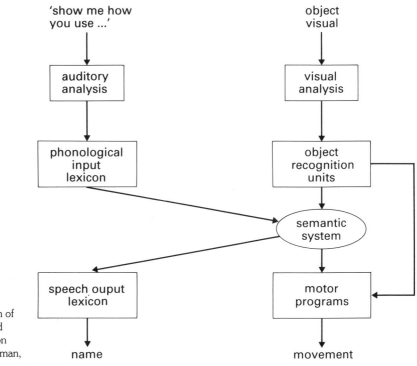

Fig. 5.5 Generation of action from visual and verbal routes (based on Rothi, Ochipa & Heilman, 1991).

Semantic system for action

Roy & Square (1985) proposed that semantic knowledge of action includes:

- knowledge of object function
- knowledge of actions into which tools and objects can be incorporated
- knowledge of sequences of actions.

Impairment of any of these components of the semantic system will result in apraxia due to the loss of the concept of action. In a single case-study by Ochipa *et al.* (1989), the patient was seen to use a spoon or a comb to brush his teeth, and a toothbrush to eat. Poor comprehension and motor deficits were eliminated. In this case the deficit was identified as poor knowledge of object function.

Direct route from vision

A single case-study of a patient with a left-hemisphere lesion resulting from a road traffic accident suggested that the motor programs of the action system can also be activated directly from the object recognition units, without access to the semantic system (Riddoch & Humphreys, 1987).

The ecological or direct theory of perception developed by Gibson (1979) emphasizes the variety of visual cues that can be picked up from the physical environment. Gibson proposed that objects 'afford' action. The 'affordance' of a surface in the environment, or of an object, is what it offers as a possibility for action. A flat surface affords sitting, a handle affords grasping, bristles afford brushing. In the performance of movement, we learn by experience that objects with certain perceptual features indicate or allow certain movements. A jug affords a sequence of filling, grasping, lifting and tipping; a brush

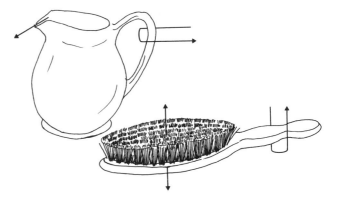

Fig. 5.6 Direct perception and action: jug 'affords' grasping, and tipping; brush 'affords' grasping, and lifting up and down.

affords grasping, and moving up and down, or side to side, as in Fig. 5.6.

The patient studied by Riddoch & Humphreys was able to match and copy pictures of objects, showing that his structural knowledge from vision was intact, but he had poor knowledge of the function of objects and he could not name them. The interesting finding of this study was that the patient, JB, could demonstrate the use of objects that he could not name. When he was given a knife and fork, for example, he could demonstrate their use even though he could not name them. Riddoch & Humphreys concluded that JB was able to activate the action system by the 'affordance' route directly from vision to action.

Verbal route

Action generated by command involves processing at the levels shown on the left-hand side of Fig. 5.5. Single case-studies have shown a dissociation between the auditory/verbal route and the visual routes to the action system. Details of these studies can be found in Rothi *et al.* (1991).

The information processing approach to the assessment of apraxia has suggested the components of the action system that may be impaired. If the component can be identified, this can suggest the types of cueing or prompting that will be beneficial. The interaction of language and perceptual processing in the motor cognitive system emphasizes the need for cooperation with the speech therapist in the assessment of dyspraxic patients.

When movement patterns related to objects are learnt, they become automatic, particularly when the activities are performed in a familiar environment. Dyspraxic patients often perform better in the home environment. The right hemiplegic patient, whose physical motor deficit has resolved, may still perform at a low level, especially if language processing is impaired.

Summary

(1) Action plans are stored as motor programs. In simple movements the motor program specifies the active muscle groups, the force, timing and direction of movement.

(2) Monitoring the progress of a movement depends on proprioceptive and visual feedback to the store of action plans. Errors may be corrected by the selection of a different motor program.

(3) In complex movements the motor program can be considered as

a generalized motor scheme which is made up of several sub-schema corresponding to the elements in the sequence of actions. Errors usually occur at transition points from one element (sub-scheme) to the next.

(4) The performance of skilled purposeful movements has been linked to the left hemisphere. Stored action memories may be located in the left parietal lobe which projects to the motor areas of the left frontal lobe for movements of the right side of the body. Learned movements of the left side of the body may be activated via the corpus callosum to the motor areas of the right frontal lobe.

(5) Information processing models of apraxia have identified access to the action system from visual, perceptual and verbal processing. Semantic knowledge of action includes the function of objects, actions related to object function, and sequencing of action. A direct non semantic route from the visual object representation to the action system for its use, has also been proposed.

References

Adam, J.A. (1971) A closed loop theory of motor behaviour. *Journal of Motor Behaviour*, **3**, 111–49.

Geschwind, N. (1975) The apraxias: neural mechanisms of disorders of learned movements. *American Scientist*, **63**, 188–95.

Gibson, J.J. (1979) *The ecological approach to visual perception.* Houghton Mifflin, Boston.

Goldberg, G. (1985) Response and projection: a reinterpretation of the premotor concept. In E.A. Roy (Ed.). Neuropsychological studies of apraxia and related disorders. Elsevier Science, Amsterdam.

Heilman, K.M., Schwartz, H.D. & Geschwind, N. (1975) Defective motor learning in ideomotor apraxia. *Neurology*,**25**, 1018–20.

Keele, S.W. (1968) Movement control in skilled motor performance. *Psychological Bulletin*, **70**, 387–403.

Lehmkuhl, G. & Poeck, K. (1981) A disturbance of the conceptual organization of actions in patients with ideational apraxia. *Cortex*, **17**, 153–8.

Ochipa, C., Rothi, L.J.G., & Heilman, K.M. (1989) Ideational apraxia: a deficit in tool selection and use. *Annals of Neurology*, **25**, 190–3.

Reason, J.T. & Mycielska, K. (1982) *Absent minded? The psychology of mental lapses and everyday errors.* Prentice-Hall, New Jersey.

Riddoch, M.J. & Humphreys, G.W. (1987) Visual object processing in a case of optic aphasia: a case of semantic access agnosia. *Cognitive Neuropsychology*, **4**, 131–85.

Rothi, L.J.G., Ochipa, C. & Heilman, K.M. (1991) A cognitive neuropsychological model of limb praxis. *Cognitive Neuropsychology*, **8**, 443–58.

Roy, E.A. & Square, P.A. (1985) Common considerations in the study of limb, verbal and oral apraxia. In E.A. Roy (Ed.) *Neuropsychological studies of apraxia and related disorders*. Elsevier Science, Amsterdam.

Schmidt, R.A. (1975) A schema theory of discrete motor skill learning. *Psychological Review*, **82**, 225–60.

Scott Kelso, J.A. (1982) (Ed.) *Human motor behaviour: an Introduction*. Lawrence Erlbaum Associates, London and Hove.

Further reading

Smyth, M.M. & Wing, A.M. (1984) *The psychology of human movement*. Academic Press, London.

Chapter 6   Attention

Attention is closely linked to perception in all human occupation. We do not perceive everything that is going on in the environment. We select some of the available stimuli for processing, while ignoring others. The playback of an audio or video tape-recorder used in a room reveals all the cues that we were not aware of at the time. The brain, on the other hand, is selecting what to listen to and what to look at from moment to moment. When there are several conversations going on at the same time we can focus our attention on one of them. However, we may also be monitoring other conversations, especially if our own name is mentioned, as in Fig. 6.1.

Fig. 6.1 The 'cocktail party phenomenon'.

At other times, we may successfully divide our attention between two or more tasks. Many students listen to music while they work, typists have meaningful conversations with colleagues whilst operating a keyboard, and parents perform household tasks and monitor the movements of children. Studies to determine how successful people are at dividing their attention have shown that there are limitations to the capacity of the brain for attentional processing.

Shifts of attention are important for flexibility in behaviour and action. When a more important event occurs attention is shifted from the current goal to a new one.

Attention has been defined in many different ways. It can refer to alertness and arousal which makes us aware of what is going on around us. We can observe alertness in others, and we experience loss of alertness in our own absent-minded behaviour. Arousal has a clear physiological basis in the activity of the reticular formation of the brain stem. Attention is also the ability to select what to focus on, and to select the responses to be made in the particular situation or circumstances.

Most of the research in cognitive psychology so far has studied attention to visual and auditory input from the external environment. Attention is also closely related to memory. Practising a task leads to more stored information, and this facilitates rapid retrieval without attention.

In neuropsychology there is increasing interest in the breakdown of attentional processing which is linked to particular brain areas. Posner & Peterson (1990) have proposed an attentional system in the brain that is anatomically separate from other systems but interacts with them for the control of mental processing. Whether this acts as a unified system in the control of all attentional processing is, at present, controversial.

The cortical areas in the attentional system are in the prefrontal cortex and the cingulate gyrus of the frontal lobes, the inferior parietal lobes and the superior temporal gyrus. These areas are part of a loop that links the reticular formation in the brain stem and the thalamus to the cerebral cortex. See Fig. 6.2.

This chapter is divided into two sections to consider the theoretical basis of two quite separate areas of dysfunction. These are:

(1) *Spatial attention* The inability to orient and attend to one side of space occurs in some stroke patients. Some of the theoretical accounts of this phenomenon of neglect will be described.

(2) *Attention in action and behaviour* A variety of problems that are commonly seen after head injury relate to attentional deficits. Some of the theoretical accounts of attention, based on studies of normal subjects, will be described; as well as some of the features of impaired attention after brain damage.

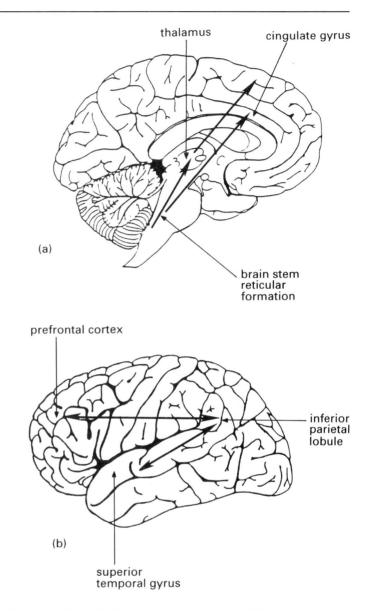

thalamus

cingulate gyrus

(a)

brain stem
reticular
formation

prefrontal cortex

inferior
parietal
lobule

(b)

superior
temporal gyrus

Fig. 6.2 The attentional system. (a) Medial view of left side of brain seen in sagittal section. (b) Side view of the left cerebral hemisphere.

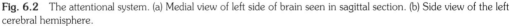

SPATIAL ATTENTION

6.1 Unilateral neglect

The phenomenon of neglect of one side of space, or unilateral neglect, is seen in some stroke patients, particularly those with right-brain damage. The patient does not search for, or respond to, stimuli in the side of space contralateral (opposite) to the lesion. The presence of unilateral neglect presents a major problem in the rehabilitation of the left hemiplegic patient. Studies in neuropsychology have shown that unilateral neglect is not a single deficit, but rather a syndrome of features that occur together. Individual patients may show different aspects of the same syndrome. The clinical features of unilateral neglect are described in Chapter 12.

Theories that have been developed to explain unilateral neglect can be divided into those that emphasize the attentional versus those that emphasize the perceptual aspects of the syndrome. There is general agreement that such neglect can be a disorder of attention, or the mental representation of space, or spatial perception.

6.1.1 Hemi-inattention

Accounts of unilateral neglect by Heilman & Valenstein (1979) and Kinsbourne (1977) have described the role of the right and left hemispheres in orienting attention to each side of space. The right hemisphere orients to the left side of space, and the left hemisphere to the right side, see Fig. 6.3. When the right side is damaged there is an imbalance in orienting. Attention is always directed to the right, mediated by the left hemisphere, and the left side of space is neglected.

Heilman extended this theory by proposing that the right hemisphere is the centre for control of arousal from the reticular formation in the brain stem. In right brain damage, the right hemisphere is under-aroused, and this further biases attention to neglect the left side.

If neglect is a disorder of attention, asking a patient to consciously report the presence of a cue on the neglected side might facilitate the

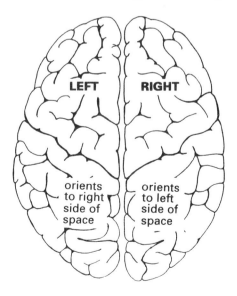

Fig. 6.3 Hemi-inattention in neglect (Heilman & Valenstein, 1985).

response to information on that side. Studies of the effects of cueing in neglect have produced conflicting results. Heilman showed no effect of cueing in patients with neglect. However, a study by Riddoch & Humphreys (1983) did show that neglect decreased when patients were forced to report a left-sided cue. These studies used a line-bisection task to test performance, see Chapter 12.

The effect of cueing was explored by Posner *et al.* (1982, 1984). In a series of experiments they investigated the effects of cueing on the response to visual stimuli presented on either side of the midline, in patients with parietal lobe, thalamic or brain stem lesions. The results of Posner's experiments showed that patients who are attending to the normal side of space (ipsilateral to the lesion) cannot disengage attention from that side, or move attention to the neglected side, or engage attention and respond to stimuli there. The three stages of (i) disengaging, (ii) moving and (iii) engaging were linked to particular brain areas in the attention system.

Cueing with coloured dots or lines on clothing, on kitchen surfaces, and on buildings on one side of a route is used in occupational therapy. The benefit of the cues may be increased if the patient consciously orients to them, so that attention is disengaged from the non-neglected side. Verbal cueing is not appropriate since it increases left hemisphere activity, which could reinforce the bias towards the right side.

6.1.2 Mental representation of space

Unilateral neglect occurs most commonly in lesion of the right parietal lobe, which plays a major role in the processing of spatial information (see Chapter 4).

A classic study of unilateral visual neglect by Bisiach *et al.* (1978) demonstrated the inability to form mental images of the affected side of space. They asked patients with left side neglect to imagine that they were in the Piazza del Duomo in Milan, which was well-known to them. Firstly, the patients were asked to imagine that they were standing in the square at the end facing the cathedral. The patients described in detail all the buildings on the right side of the square, but the buildings on the left were omitted. When the patients were next asked to imagine that they were standing at the opposite end of the square on the steps of the cathedral, they described all the buildings that they had neglected before, and omitted the buildings that were now on the left side. Bisiach suggested that in unilateral neglect there is an inability to form a mental representation of the left side of space, which is used in visuospatial perception as well as in forming a mental image. Later experiments, which showed that patients can improve their descriptions of the neglected side if they are cued to do so, gave more support to the attentional account of neglect.

6.1.3 Spatial attention in personal and extrapersonal space

The fractionation of space into three areas, which can be called personal, reaching and locomotor space (see Fig. 4.3), has been supported by studies of patients with unilateral neglect. There may be selective impairment of attention in one of these areas and not in the others. For example, a patient in a wheelchair who consistently bumps into obstacles on the left side may have neglect of locomotor space, but may have no problems in self-care activities in personal space. A single case-study by Halligan & Marshall (1991), using a conventional test (see Chapter 12, Section 12.1), showed unilateral neglect of reaching space but not in locomotor space. As part of a study of twenty-six patients with right brain damage, performance of self-care activities in personal space was compared with the use of objects in reaching space, (Zocolatti & Judica, 1991). The results showed that performance using items in relation to body parts on the neglected side was less impaired than items manipulated in reaching space. A single case-study by the same authors showed the opposite effect, namely unilateral neglect of personal space with unimpaired reaching space. Neglect of personal space may be related to loss of awareness of body parts (anosognosia), see Chapter 10, Section 10.3.1.

Other accounts of neglect have described the inability to initiate movement into the neglected side of space. Heilman called this akinesia, which is not a motor deficit, but a loss of the intention to act. Poor exploration of contralateral space can also result from oculomotor disturbances, in which the patient cannot visually scan the neglected side.

The different accounts of unilateral neglect reported in the literature seem to confirm that it is not a unitary phenomenon. Deficits in attentional processing, spatial perception, body scheme and the planning of movements to the opposite side of space may all contribute to the neglect syndrome. The clinical picture is varied, both in detail of symptoms and in the prognosis. In some patients the condition resolves in a few days, in others in a few months. The persistence of severe unilateral neglect is a major factor in the failure of left-hemiplegic patients to respond to rehabilitation (Denes *et al.*, 1982).

Summary

(1) Brain damage, particularly of the right side, can result in the inability to orient to stimuli on the side of space opposite to the lesion. Theories that account for this phenomenon of unilateral neglect include:

(i) A disorder of attention. Each cerebral hemisphere orients attention to the opposite side of space, and in addition, the right hemisphere controls arousal originating in the brain stem. If one hemisphere is damaged, there is loss of automatic response to stimuli on the opposite side, and the effect is more marked with right hemisphere lesions.

(ii) A disorder of the mental representation of space. The right hemisphere is dominant for spatial processing, and unilateral neglect may originate from the inability to form a mental representation of the opposite side of space.

(2) The functional evaluation of spatial attention in patients with unilateral neglect has shown that spatial attention may be divided into three areas: personal, reaching and locomotor space. Selective impairment of attention can occur in each of the three areas in unilateral neglect.

ATTENTION IN ACTION AND BEHAVIOUR

The attentional problems that occur after cerebral damage include the inability to focus attention on the task in hand, and to shift attention from one action or event to another. Tasks that demand high mental effort become difficult and those that were formerly automatic now demand conscious attentional control. Some of the theories of attention that relate to these problems will now be considered.

6.2 Focused attention

Focused attention is the ability to process one input and ignore others. Psychologists studying focused attention in the 1950s investigated auditory attention using dichotic listening experiments. The subjects wore headphones and different messages were played into each ear simultaneously. In some experiments the subjects were asked to recall the input to one ear and ignore the other. In other trials, when they were asked to recall the input from both ears, the recall showed that they were switching attention from one ear to the other, and they never mixed up the two messages.

Two different information processing models were developed from dichotic listening studies. One model, based on Broadbent (1958), suggested that filtering occurs at an early stage of sensory registration and only one input is allowed to pass on for perceptual and semantic analysis. The filtered inputs may be held in a temporary store for later processing. An alternative model (Deutsch & Deutsch, 1963) proposed that selection occurs at a later stage, after the perceptual processing of all inputs. Then only one input passes on to produce the

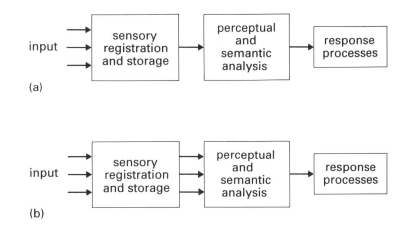

Fig. 6.4 (a) Early and (b) late selection of theories of attention.

response, based on its relevance in the particular situation. Figure 6.4 shows the difference between these early and late selection theories. Whether the selection of inputs occurs early or late in processing may depend on how easy it is to discriminate between them.

Experiments in visual attention have shown that early parallel processing of the features of objects in the environment, for example, colour, size and shape, occurs automatically without attention. A second stage combines these features to form an object which can be recognized, and this stage does require focused attention (Triesman & Gelade, 1980). This process has been compared to a spotlight that focuses attention on the features to be combined at a particular location. Focused visual attention moving from one location to another is involved in many work tasks, such as monitoring instruments and proof-reading.

A crucial feature in all task performance is the ability to select and focus on information that is relevant to the task, while ignoring background stimuli. Some patients with attentional problems have difficulty in filtering irrelevant stimuli. Other patients are not able to sustain the focus of attention demanded by the task and passively shift attention to other things.

6.3 Attention capacity

In everyday experience we are able to shift attention from one task to another and to do two things at the same time. Psychologists have investigated how attention can be allocated between all the demands at any one time. Kahneman (1973) proposed a central processor of attention with a limited capacity. The allocation of attentional resources occurs in parallel, and depends on the demands of the particular activities. Kahneman's model regards attention as a dynamic process that constantly evaluates the demands of task performance. The central allocation policy monitors the resources needed to perform more than one task at a time, as in Fig. 6.5.

The demands on attentional capacity vary in several ways:

(i)   *Mental effort.* Tasks that involve high mental effort demand a large share of the total attention capacity
(ii)   *Skill.* The acquisition of skill at a task, as a result of practice, reduces the attention demands, so that more is available to attend to other tasks.
(iii) *Motivation* and *arousal* increase the total capacity available for allocation.

Studies of normal subjects doing two tasks at a time have been used to investigate the capacity theory. Splelke, Hirst & Neisser (1976) gave two students the difficult dual task of reading a short story for comprehension at the same time as they wrote down words dictated to them. At first, their speed of reading was slow, and their handwriting was poor. After six weeks of training for five hours a week, they were able to read with speed and understanding at the same time as writing to dictation.

Dual task experiments of this kind demonstrate a remarkable ability to divide attention between two tasks. When both tasks have high processing demands, new strategies for performing each task may develop, so that there is less interference between them. There is less interference between two tasks that use different modalities; for

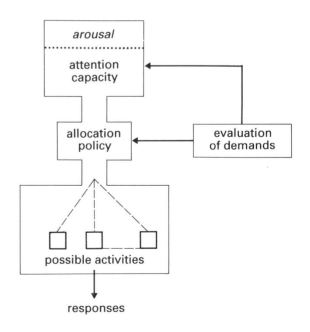

Fig. 6.5 Capacity model of attention (simplified from Kahneman, 1973).

example, listening to the radio whilst writing is easier than listening to the radio at the same time as holding a conversation.

You can assess your own ability to do more than one thing at a time as follows:

Activity

Watch your favourite soap or situation comedy on the television with a friend. At the same time, you copy our your notes from a lecture that day. At the end of the program, recall the details of what happened in the TV program to your friend, and ask him/her to question you on the content of the lecture.

If you have had the experience of learning to drive, recall the changes in the attention demands of this task. At first, driving required high mental effort, and all your attention was directed to the task. Once the skill of driving was acquired, attention could be allocated to talk to a passenger, or to listen to the radio.

Attention capacity may be reduced after brain damage. Tasks that require high mental effort may become difficult, while tasks that are well learned and familiar are easier. General arousal may be reduced so that performance is slow and concentration is required in all activities.

6.4 Automatic and controlled processing

It is common experience that well- learned and practised activities become automatic. All routine and habitual activities and behaviours are done on 'auto pilot'. In the presence of an environmental cue or cues, a task is planned and completed without any apparent need for conscious control. All new learning experience, on the other hand, requires controlled attention and relies on feedback about performance.

The difference between automatic and controlled processing was studied by Shiffrin & Schneider (1977) using laboratory-based visual tasks. In these experiments, it was shown that:

- automatic processes are fast, do not require attention, but they are difficult to modify;
- controlled processes are relatively slow, demand attention, but they are flexible when circumstances change.

These studies distinguished two types of processing that occur in tasks involving visual attention, but did not explain how processing changes from controlled to automatic as a result of practice.

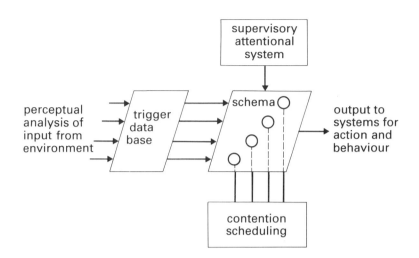

Fig. 6.6 Model of automatic and controlled attention (based on Shallice, 1982).

A computer-based model of automatic and controlled processes was developed by Norman & Shallice (Shallice, 1982), shown in Fig. 6.6. Practise of routine activities leads to stored memory representations or 'schema'. Each scheme is activated in response to particular inputs from the environment. A scheme for answering the telephone is activated by recognition of the sound of the phone ringing. A scheme for dressing will contain sub-routines for each garment of clothing.

The model includes a mechanism for inhibition of all conflicting schema when one scheme is activated. This means that routine action and behaviour can be performed automatically without interference. The selection of the appropriate scheme, and inhibition of all others is called contention scheduling.

When a novel situation is presented in the environment, the selection of a scheme is controlled by a supervisory attention system. Controlled processing by this system is also involved when decision-making is required. If the supervisory system is impaired, inappropriate action may be activated by automatic processing. The loss of controlled attention leads to distractability and perseveration.

There is neuropsychological evidence that the supervisory attentional system is located in the frontal lobe. This high-level control of attention is involved in all aspects of problem solving, whereby action and behaviour are planned and modified flexibly from one pattern to another. The supervisory system can be impaired independently from the attentional processing in routine tasks (Shallice, 1982).

Summary

(1) Focused attention allows some sensory inputs to be processed, while others are ignored. From all the sensory inputs impinging

on the brain in parallel, the selection of those for conscious attention may occur early in perceptual processing or after the analysis for meaning has occurred. The ability to focus attention on task-relevant information is crucial in all functional activities.

(2) Capacity theories of attention describe a central resource of attention capacity that is allocated in parallel between various tasks. Attention demands are lowest when a task requires low mental effort, and is well-learned and practised. Attention capacity is increased when the level of arousal is high.

(3) An information processing model that distinguishes habitual and routine action and behaviour from the responses to novel situations, has been proposed. The model includes a supervisory attentional system, located in the frontal lobe, that plans and regulates responses to novel situations and is the basis of problem solving activity.

References

Spatial attention

Bisiach, E. & Luzatti, C. (1978) Unilateral neglect of representational space. Cortex, **14**, 129–33.

Denes, G., Semenza, C., Stoppa, E. & Lis, A. (1982). Unilateral spatial neglect and recovery from hemiplegia. A follow-up study. *Brain*, **105**, 543–52.

Halligan, P.W. & Marshall, J.C. (1991) Left neglect for near but not far space in man. *Nature*, **350**, 498–500.

Heilman, K.M. & Valenstein, E. (1985) *Clinical Neuropsychology.* Oxford University Press, New York.

Kinsbourne, M. (1977) Hemineglect and hemisphere rivalry. In E.A. Weinstein & R.P. Friedland (Eds) *Advances in Neurology.* Raven Press, New York.

Posner, M.I. & Peterson, S.E. (1990) The attentional system of the human brain. *Annual Review of Neuroscience*, **13** 25–42.

Posner, M.I., Cohen, Y. & Rafal, R.D. (1982) Neural systems control of spatial orienting. *Philosophical Transactions of the Royal Society of London*, **B 298**, 187–98.

Posner, M.I., Walker, J.A., Friedrich, F.J. & Rafal, R.D. (1984) Effects of parietal injury on covert orienting of visual attention. *Journal of Neuroscience*, **4**, 1863–74.

Riddoch, M.J. & Humphreys, G.W. (1983) The effect of cueing on unilateral neglect. *Neuropsychologica*, **21**, 589–99.

Zoccolatti, P. & Judica, A. (1991) Functional evaluation of hemineglect by means of a semi-structured scale. *Neuropsychological Rehabilitation*, **1**, 33–44.

Attention in action and behaviour

Broadbent, D. (1958) *Perception and Communication.* Pergamon, Oxford.

Deutsch, J.A. & Deutsch, D. (1963) Attention: some theoretical considerations. *Psychological Review*, **80**, 80–90.

Kahneman, D. (1973) Attention and Effort. Prentice-Hall, New Jersey.

Shallice, T. (1982) Specific impairments of planning. *Philosophical Transactions of the Royal Society of London,* **B 298**, 199–209.

Shiffrin, R.M. & Schneider, W. (1977) Controlled and automatic human information processing: II. Perceptual learning, automatic attending, and a general theory. *Psychological Review*, **84**, 127–190.

Spelke, E.S., Hirst, W.C. & Neisser, U. (1976) Skills of divided attention. *Cognition*, **4**, 215–30.

Treisman, A.M. & Gelade, G. (1980) A feature integration theory of attention. *Cognitive Psychology*, **12**, 97–136.

Further reading

Eysenck, M.W. & Keane, M.T. (1990) Cognitive Psychology: A student's handbook. Lawrence Erlbaum, London.

Chapter 4, Attention and performance limitations.

Smyth, M.M., Morris, P.E. Levy, P. & Ellis, A.W. (1987) Cognition in Action. Lawrence Erlbaum, London.

Chapter 5. Tapping your head and rubbing your stomach: Doing two things at once.

Chapter 7   Memory

Fig. 7.1 Information storage and retrieval.

Memory is our ability to keep things in mind, and to recall them at some time in the future. Accounts of memory in psychology consider how items are registered, the organization of the material that is stored, and the mental processing involved in its retrieval. Attention and perception are particularly related to memory. We must perceive and attend to an item before it can be remembered.

Memory is often compared with systems that organize and store large amounts of information. A library of books is a static store of information that has been organized in a particular way, but retrieval is slow, see Fig. 7.1.

Today, by sitting at a computer anywhere in the world, we can gain rapid retrieval of knowledge that is continually being updated, as long as the computer has been programmed for access. Similarly, normal memory is an information system that is constantly changing, and its use depends on easy access.

For a long time investigations of memory in psychology were laboratory-based, so that conditions for presentation and subsequent recall of the items to be remembered could be carefully controlled and varied in a predetermined way. The results of such rigorous explorations of memory, using lists of digits, letters or words, have produced models of mental processing in memory. Laboratory-based studies of patients with memory impairment have supported and extended these models.

From the 1970s onwards, investigations of memory have included material that is related to everyday experiences; for example pictures, stories, maps and videos. In addition, self-report questionnaires have been used in which subjects are asked to record what they remember and what they forget. The studies of memory in everyday experience are largely concerned with the contents of memory, rather than with the mechanisms involved.

The neuroanatomical approach to memory has identified the location of lesion sites in patients with neurological disorders that cause severe amnesia. These studies have shown that many areas are involved, and that they are widely distributed in the brain. It follows that some impairment of memory occurs in most patients with brain damage, but it also explains why global amnesia is not common. The brain areas that have been identified in different types of memory loss are given in Chapter 13.

Patients with memory deficits do have residual memory skills. Their prospects for rehabilitation may largely depend on the identification and development of the spared memory. Occupational therapists have the opportunity to assess and monitor memory problems that relate to functional ability (Robinson, 1992).

Memory can be broadly divided into short-term, or working, memory for the temporary storage of information, and long-term memory which holds information for long periods of time.

7.1 Short-term memory

Short-term memory holds information just long enough for us to use it. We are aware of using the short-term memory when we look up a telephone number and remember it long enough to dial the number. There are, however, many other activities that demand a temporary store of information that soon becomes lost. Our ability to hold a conversation depends on the retention of several words long enough to remember what has been said, and another group of words prior to speaking them. We manipulate groups of numbers to sort out the change in shopping. If we drive along an unknown road or enter an unfamiliar supermarket, it seems likely that 'snapshots' of visual and spatial information are held for a short time to allow us to find our way. Miller (1956) proposed the 'magical number seven, plus or minus two' items for the capacity of the short-term memory store. These items can be numbers, letters, words or short phrases. They are often referred to as 'chunks' or units of information.

The separation of a short-term (or primary) memory store was part of the multistore model of memory, see Fig. 7.2, described in Atkinson & Shiffrin (1971).

The model describes three memory systems:

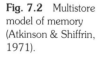

Fig. 7.2 Multistore model of memory (Atkinson & Shiffrin, 1971).

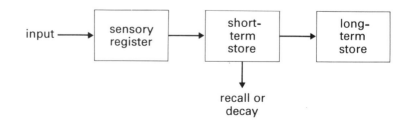

- *Sensory memory* is the brief processing of information received by the sense organs that lasts only a few milliseconds. Sensory memory includes visual (iconic), auditory (echoic), tactile and proprioceptive input. So far there have been few studies of tactile and proprioceptive sensory memory in psychology. Sensory memory allows for further analysis of the stimulus in each modality.
- *Short-term memory* holds information from the sensory store for several seconds. This allows rehearsal before activating a response, or before passing on to long-term memory.
- *Long-term memory* holds information for periods of time from a few minutes to many years.

The evidence for a short term memory store is based on the results of free recall of a list of numbers, letters or words.

Activity

Make a list of 15 words. Choose concrete nouns rather than abstract words or adjectives.

Read the list to a group of colleagues at about one word per second. Then ask them to write down the words in the list that they recall. Check the position in the list of each word recalled by each person.

Repeat with another list, and this time give the group a short exercise in mental arithmetic to do before writing down the words they remember. Again check each recalled word for its position in the list.

The words most frequently recalled will probably be those at the end of the list. This is known as the recency effort. When the recall was delayed, and the mental arithmetic task was added before recall, the recency effect disappeared.

The recency effect, explored in controlled laboratory conditions, supports the presence of a limited capacity short-term memory store which holds the last few items. If recall is delayed and rehearsal is prevented by asking the subjects to do another task before recall, then the recency effect disappears. The early items in the list (primacy effect) show no change in recall performance as they have already entered the long term store.

One limitation of the multistore model is that information can only enter long-term memory via the short-term store. Later versions of the model included some coding for meaning in the short-term memory, and some retrieval of items from the long-term store into short-term memory.

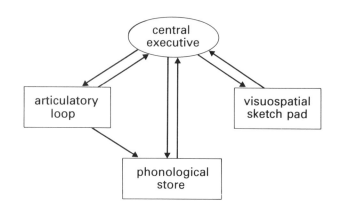

Fig. 7.3 Working memory model.

7.2 Working memory

The working memory model (Baddeley 1986) was developed to replace the single, passive short-term store by a range of temporary stores, controlled by an attentional system called the central executive, see Fig. 7.3.

In this model some active processing of information occurs as well as temporary storage. Numbers may be held long enough for some manipulation in mental arithmetic. The meaning and syntax of word phrases required for fluent speech are also processed.

The *articulatory loop* (inner voice) holds and rehearses items in the same order that they are presented, like an audio tape that can be replayed for around two seconds. In this loop items are held in the *phonological store* which has a limited capacity. Information can also enter the phonological store from the long-term memory, for example, in the recall of names during conversation.

The *visuospatial sketch* (scratch) *pad* (or inner eye) holds both spatial information and visual images that cannot be rehearsed verbally, such as size, shape and colour. This temporary store can also be used to inspect and manipulate visual images from long-term memory. When driving or cycling along a route we may recall in turn particular parts of the visual scene.

The *central executive* is an attentional system with limited capacity. It directs the allocation of attention to both visual and verbal aspects of a task, and controls the processing in all the components of working memory. The central executive is particularly important when the cognitive demands of a task are high, for example if we are talking to a friend while we are trying to use the phone.

The working memory model offers a more comprehensive account of the functions of short term memory in daily life. Also the various deficits identified in patients with impairment of short-term memory can only be explained by the presence of several short-term memory systems.

7.3 Long-term memory

Studies of long term memory in cognitive psychology have described the ways in which information is organized in the long-term memory, which has unlimited capacity. There is evidence for the separation of more than one system in the long-term memory. This has been supported by the selective impairment of different parts of the system in patients with memory loss.

7.3.1 Overview of the structure of long-term memory

A distinction between three different types of long-term memory was first proposed by Tulving (1972), see Fig. 7.4.

- *Episodic* memory is a system that retains memories which are linked to a time and a place. These are autobiographical memories, such as where you spent your holiday last year, or the first trip you made by plane.
- *Semantic* memory is a system of general knowledge acquired over time and unrelated to the events at the time of learning. We know that Rome is the capital of Italy, bananas are yellow, and so on.
- *Procedural* memory is a system of information that cannot be inspected consciously. Motor skills that we have learnt are part of procedural memory. We remember how to swim, to ride a bike, to drive a golf ball accurately, but we cannot explain in detail how we do it. Also, speaking our first language is part of procedural memory, and most of us cannot explain the complicated rules of grammar associated with it.

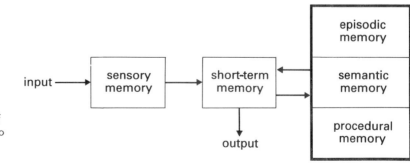

Fig. 7.4 Divisions of long-term memory into semantic, episodic, procedural memory.

One of the major arguments for the separation of episodic and semantic memory has been the study of patients with amnesia. These patients, typically, cannot remember what happened a short time ago (episodic memory), but their general knowledge from semantic memory remains intact (Parkin, 1982). However, some episodic memories from the past can be remembered, and one of the main problems in amnesia is the inability to learn new information. For example, the names of people met since the onset cannot be learnt, and there is poor recognition of pictures of people who have become famous in recent times. There is now more evidence to suggest that some episodic and semantic memory from the past is retained, but amnesics have poor memory for both episodic and semantic information following the onset of memory loss.

In normal memory, stored episodic and semantic information interact and may change over time. Learning to use a microcomputer may at first be associated with a particular model in a college laboratory (episodic). After a time, the operation of the computer becomes part of our general knowledge in semantic memory.

The overlap between semantic and episodic memory led Cohen & Squire (1980) to suggest that both systems are combined in what they called *declarative memory*. This memory system requires conscious access for retrieval of information and was described as 'knowing that'. Procedural memory, on the other hand, is 'knowing how' and we can perform habitual activities and skills without conscious recall from memory. Procedural memory is spared in most patients with memory loss, so that skills well-learned before its onset are retained. This has important implications for the return to work in memory-impaired individuals.

The separation of memory systems with and without awareness is supported by recent studies of amnesic patients. It has been shown that some amnesic patients can learn new skills (Graf & Schacter, 1985) and can recall information even though they are not aware of it. Tests of memory are usually measures of explicit memory, and give only a limited insight into memory function. Further research into the ways in which spared implicit memory can be exploited by memory-impaired patients may lead to further accounts of the explicit (declarative) and implicit (non declarative) components of long-term memory. A summary of the ways in which the memory system is organized is given in Fig. 7.5.

7.3.2 Processing in long-term memory

Three stages of processing occur in long-term memory:

- Coding or registration of information as a memory trace at the time of learning.

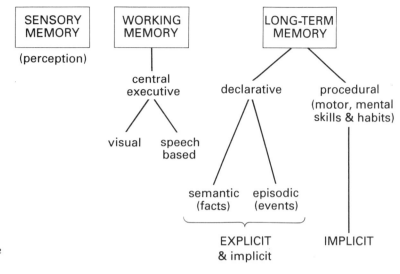

Fig. 7.5 Summary of the structure of memory.

- Storage or retention of memory traces over time. This is a dynamic process changing as new information is organized with what has already been learnt.
- Retrieval of information when it is required by activation of the correct memory trace.

All these processes are essential for memory function. Some of the theories of long-term memory will be outlined under the headings of registration, retention and retrieval.

Registration in memory

The registration or coding of information is the processing that occurs at the time of learning. This aspect of memory has been explored by manipulating the features and the context of information that is learnt, and testing the subsequent recall to see what factors are most important.

Craik & Lockhart (1972) showed that the strength of the memory trace depends on the level or depth of processing at the time of learning. Depth is defined as the amount of meaning associated with the information. The benefit of deep processing on subsequent recall could also be due to elaboration of the memory trace. In deep processing, more information is coded in the memory trace, and this leads to easier access in the memory system. I am more likely to remember a student's name if I also learn his/her home town and previous occupation, than if I just register his/her physical appearance.

The benefits of deep processing and elaboration of the information can be applied to the strategies we use to improve memory. Students who acquire anatomical knowledge by rote learning are usually less successful than those whose learning is related to function.

Retention in memory

Once a memory trace has been registered, subsequent forgetting could be the result of decay of the trace over time, or interference of the trace by later learning. Laboratory experiments have clearly demonstrated that recall of items is worse after intervened learning of similar items, compared with merely resting in the interval before recall. In everyday experience, if we are asked to recall a particular event, it is more difficult to search memory for one particular example of many similar events. Baddeley & Hitch (1977) asked Rugby football players to remember the teams they had played against in the previous season. Recall success did not depend on the elapsed time but on the number of intervening matches for each player. This suggests that forgetting was due to interference, rather than the time that had elapsed.

In Alzheimer's and Korsakoff's diseases there is a loss of cholinergic neurotransmitter substances in the brain (Kopelman, 1986). Since poor learning of new material is characteristic of these neurological conditions, the loss of neurotransmitters has been linked to poor registration and storage in memory. More research into the effect of drugs that stimulate the production of these transmitters may confirm this.

Retrieval in memory

The benefit of cueing to aid the retrieval of items from memory is a well-known phenomenon.

Recall is the most difficult retrieval process. In recall, we remember without any additional information to assist us. An example might be, 'Do you know the name of the head occupational therapist (OT) at a named hospital?'

Cued recall makes the task easier, when we are given some information to assist us. For example, 'Do you know the name of the head OT at a named hospital? Her initials are AL.'

Recognition is the retrieval process that shows the highest level of performance. You are given the names or photographs of five head OTs and you are asked, 'Which one is the head OT at the named hospital?' We are all familiar with the 'tip-of-the-tongue phenomenon' when we know an item is in memory but we cannot retrieve it. When the item is presented, we instantly recognize it.

Retrieval is affected by context and mood. Items are more likely to be retrieved in the same environment as learning. Godden &

Baddeley (1975) showed that recall is better when environment at learning is the same as that at recall, although a later experiment showed less effect of context on recognition. Memory training in hospital may not generalize to the home environment. Experimental studies of the effects of drugs have shown that learning in the altered state can be recalled better in the same state. Depressed patients easily recall memories of sad events and this can add to their depression (Teasdale, 1983).

7.4 Everyday memory

The way that a person's memory functions depends largely on life experience and on the particular cognitive demands on that person in daily living. Running a home, working as an accounts clerk, and playing darts or chess, all use memory in different ways. Normal memory is not globally good or globally bad. People are good at remembering some things and bad at others; the pattern is variable.

One feature of everyday memory is the variety of strategies that normal subjects use to remember things.

Activity _____

Try the memory exercise of Kim's Game with a group of friends by placing eight objects on a tray with a cover over them.

Uncover the items for one minute and then ask the group to write down the objects they remember.

Discuss the strategies that each member of the group used to try to memorize the objects

---

You probably found that some people tried to memorize the position of each object on the tray, others grouped those of the same colour or the same function, and yet more tried to make a first letter mnemonic for the objects with varying success.

Another feature of normal memory function is the variety of external memory aids used by different people. A survey of a group of university students and a group of housewives was carried out by Harris (1980). He gave the subjects a checklist of memory aids and asked them to record how often they used each one on a rating scale of 0 (never used) to 6 (used eleven or more times in the last two weeks). A sample from the list is given in Table 7.1.

Table 7.1 What memory aids do you use? (After Harris 1980.)

(1) Shopping lists
(2) Diary
(3) Writing on hand
(4) Alarm clock for waking up only
(5) Clock timer for cooking
(6) Alarm watch for purposes other than waking and cooking
(7) Memos – lists of things to be done (work/home)
(8) Wall charts, year planners
(9) First-letter memory aids
(10) Rhymes
(11) Mentally retrace a sequence of events or actions
(12) Turning numbers into letters
(13) Face/name associations
(14) Alphabetical searching (name begins with?)
(15) Ask other people to remember things for you
(16) Leave objects in special places to act as reminders
(17) Pegwood method for a list – 'one is stop, two is look . . .'
(18) Story method – make up story connecting items in order
(19) Place method – imagine a series of familiar places

Activity

Try this list on a group of friends and discuss the variation you find within the group.

In the study by Harris high ratings were given to an appointments diary, and to mentally retracing a sequence of events or actions to remember where you lost something.

Everyday memory is remembering to do things, as well as remembering information from the past. Most of the studies of memory have been concerned with memory that is retrospective. *Prospective memory*, on the other hand, is remembering to act in the future without obvious external cues. Failures in prospective memory occur when we forget to put an important letter in the post on the way home, or forget to telephone a friend on his/her birthday. External memory aids are most useful for prospective memory.

For the memory-impaired person, prospective memory may include remembering to do all self-care activities, or to meet a friend on time. Prospective memory loss may have the most significant effect on the ability to function independently. More research is needed into methods of assessing prospective memory, and evaluation of the strategies that can be used to overcome it.

Summary

(1) The working memory model is an account of how information from the environment can be held for short periods of time. Both verbal (speech based) and visual information is rehearsed before passing on to long-term memory. Information retrieved from long-term memory is processed in working memory for recall.

(2) Long-term memory includes three stages of processing:
  (i) Registration of items or events at the time of learning. The strength of the memory trace depends on and the level of processing, elaboration and context.
  (ii) Retention of memory traces may be more affected by interference than by decay with time.
  (iii) Retrieval processes access stored memories. Retrieval can be achieved with or without awareness, and it is affected by context and mood.

(3) The organization of long-term memory can be divided into:
  (i) Declarative memory for facts and events, that is retrieved by conscious awareness.
  (ii) Procedural memory for learned skills, that does not involve conscious access.

(4) Severe memory impairment, in the absence of intellectual deterioration, is characterized by an inability to learn new information or to recall recent events. Some episodic memories and semantic knowledge from the past are retained. Procedural memory is usually spared.

(5) Memory function in everyday experience is related to the cognitive demands made on the particular individual. Prospective memory, which plays an important role in everyday memory, is an important area for future research.

References

Atkinson, R.C. & Shiffrin, R.M. (1971) The control of short-term memory. *Scientific American*, **225**, 82–90.

Baddeley, A.D. (1986) *Working Memory*. Oxford University Press, Oxford.

Baddeley, A.D. & Hitch, G.J. (1977) In A. Baddeley (1992) *Your memory. A user's guide*. Penguin Books, London.

Craik, F.I.M. & Lockhart, R.S. (1972) Levels of processing: a framework for memory research. *Journal of verbal learning and verbal behaviour*, **11**, 671–84.

Godden, D. & Baddeley, A.D. (1975) Context dependent memory in two natural environments: on land and under water. *British Journal of Psychology*, **66**, 325–31.

Graf, P. & Schachter, D.L. (1985) Implicit and explicit memory for new associations in normal and amnesic subjects. *Journal of Experimental Psychology: Learning, Memory and Cognition*, **10**, 164–78.

Harris, J.E. (1980a) Memory aids people use: two interview studies. *Memory and cognition*, **8**, 31–8.

Kopelman, M.D. (1986) The cholinergic neurotransmitter system in human memory and dementia: a review. *Quarterly Journal of Experimental Psychology*, **38a**, 535–74.

Miller, G.A. (1956) The magic number seven, plus or minus two: some limits on our capacity for processing information. *Psychological Review*, **63**, 81–97.

Parkin, A.J. (1982) Residual learning capacity in organic amnesia. *Cortex*, **18**, 417–40.

Robinson, S. (1992) Occupational therapy in a memory clinic. *British Journal of Occupational Therapy*, **55** 394–6.

Teasdale, J.D. (1983) Affect and accessibility. *Philosophical Transactions of the Royal Society of London*, **B 302**, 403–12.

Tulving, E. (1972) Episodic and semantic memory. In E. Tulving & W. Donaldson (Eds) Organization of Memory. Academic Press, London.

Further reading

Baddeley, A. (1992) *Your Memory: a user's guide.* Penguin Books, London.

Cohen, G. Eysenck, M.W. & Le Voi, M.E. (1986) *Memory: a cognitive approach.* Open University Press, Milton Keynes.

Part III   Assessment of Perception and Cognition in Occupational Therapy

Chapter 8 Introduction to Assessment

8.1 The role of assessment in the treatment process

The range of assessments for neurologically impaired patients in occupational therapy cover social, emotional and cognitive aspects of behaviour, in both individuals and groups. Some assessments relate specifically to neurological function – for example, muscle tone, reflexes, sensation and perception. Other assessments are concerned with task performance in daily living, work and leisure activities. Assessment has a role in all stages of the treatment process, see Fig. 8.1: observation; intervention; and evaluation.

Observation

Observation in the early stages identifies functional problems. If an observation is structured in a formal way, it can then be called an *Assessment*. The recorded structure of an assessment allows the same procedure to be repeated on another occasion, and by another therapist, for comparison. Assessment elaborates observation, and can identify covert problems which may not be apparent to the observer. This is particularly true in perceptual and cognitive function.

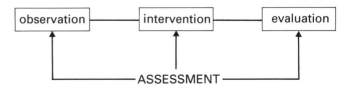

Fig. 8.1   Treatment process.

A patient may be unable to complete a task for a variety of reasons. He or she may have poor concentration or poor motivation, or there may be deficits in visual perception or sequencing. Observations and assessments made by relatives and carers can also contribute to the process, particularly for patients with cognitive problems.

The early stages of assessment form a basis for the planning of intervention, and for setting realistic goals.

Intervention

In some treatment programmes assessments are part of treatment, particularly when it involves regular practice at a functional task. For example, in dressing practice, the stage reached each day forms an assessment which gives feedback to the therapist and to the patient.

Evaluation

The repetition of assessments throughout all stages of treatment forms one method of evaluation. Changes in the assessment results over time give a measure of the response to treatment, over and above spontaneous recovery.

In the acute hospital setting, the emphasis is on the return to independence, and occupational therapy is usually focused on self-care and on the various aspects of physical disability. The residual disabilities often include perceptual and cognitive problems. These may remain with the patient for the rest of their lives, and relate to both future work prospects and leisure pursuits.

Rehabilitation in the community provides the opportunity for the assessment of the client in the home environment where cognitive problems that were absent in the structured environment of the hospital may now be encountered.

8.2 Pre-assessment tasks

The following may be used as a useful check-list with a patient before deciding whether to complete a standardized assessment of perception and cognition.

- Has the patient been assessed recently by another therapist?
- Do you fully understand the validation criteria of the assessment?
- Establish the patient's hand dominance.
- Assess motor ability. The patient may be unable to manipulate objects, or to use a pencil for drawing.
- Check eyesight – glasses for reading?

- Ask for pre-test screening by the speech therapist.
- Assessment of pre-morbid IQ from:
  - ○ previous education and experience
  - ○ information from relatives
  - ○ National Adult Reading Test (Nelson, 1982).
- Is English a second language for the patient? Some tests require knowledge of written and spoken English.
- Assessment of attention span – visual and auditory, particularly in early CVAs and head injuries.
- Assess the patient's attitude to the test and anxiety level.
- Look at the CAT scan result, if available.
- Complete the test in a suitable environment, quiet and comfortable.

Do not forget that you are assessing from a baseline of normal.

(Adams, J. 1991)

8.3 Standardized tests of perception and cognition

Four standardized tests that are appropriate for use in occupational therapy will be included in this section. They are:

- The Rivermead Perceptual Assessment Battery (RPAB).
- The Chessington Occupational Therapy Neurological Assessment Battery (COTNAB).
- The Rivermead Behavioural Memory Battery (RBMT)
- The Behavioural Inattention Test (BIT).

Each of these batteries, summarized in Appendix 2, has been standardized on normal subjects. The RPAB has also been standardized on a group of elderly with no neurological impairments. Each test is scored, and the total score gives an estimate of overall performance which can be graded by comparison with scores from normal subjects of the same age and pre-morbid IQ.

There are advantages and disadvantages for standardized tests for the following reasons.

Advantages

- The tests are objective.
- There is a clear procedure for the administration of each test.
- Tests can be repeated on the same patient at different times to show progress.
- Different therapists can assess the same patient, and reliable comparisons can be made.
- Performance by one patient can be compared with other patients in the same or different departments.

- The results can be used to support and extend functional assessments.

Disadvantages

- Good patient cooperation is required.
- Some patients may not be able to complete the whole battery on one occasion without fatigue.
- Tests are mainly static displays without any time dimension and are presented in the absence of context.
- It is difficult to administer some of the tests to patients with receptive language problems.

Observation of the patient's behaviour during the tests can be as important as the actual scores (Jesshope *et al.*, 1991). Repetition of the test gives the opportunity for the therapist to observe changes in behaviour, and can show progress, if any, to the patient. The individual test scores can be used as a basis for further investigation, and to predict functional problems.

8.3.1 The Rivermead Perceptual Assessment Battery (RPAB)

(Whiting, Lincoln, Bhavnani & Cockburn, 1985)

This test was designed for the assessment of visual and spatial perception by occupational therapists. The RPAB provides a good initial test for the screening of all patients with neurological impairment. Perceptual problems which need further assessment in functional activities can be identified.

There are sixteen perceptual tests that can be grouped into eight areas:

(i)   Form constancy
(ii)   Colour constancy
(iii)   Sequencing
(iv)   Object completion
(v)   Figure ground discrimination
(vi)   Body image
(vii)   Inattention
(viii) Spatial awareness.

The original test was standardized on normal subjects aged 16 to 69 years (Cockburn *et al.*, 1982), and validated on a group of stroke and head injury patients. A further standard for the elderly aged 65 to 92 years has been added.

The complete test takes around one hour to administer. This is not always possible due to patient fatigue or constraints on the therapist's time. If the full test is used in the order indicated in the test manual, the assessment could be stopped when a patient fails four or more consecutive tests. Severe perceptual deficits can be identified in this way, but the whole battery of tests needs to be completed in patients with mild perceptual problems. Studies in the literature have taken failure on three (Jesshope *et al.*, 1991) or four (Edmans & Lincoln, 1987) of the subtests to indicate the presence of perceptual problems.

Lincoln & Edmans (1989) investigated the possibility of a shortened version of the RPAB by analysing the scores on all the tests in 169 normal subjects and 190 stroke patients. The results of the analysis produced three different shortened versions of eight tests each. The shortened versions take 35 minutes to administer on average. Version A consists of 4 visuospatial and 4 matching tests. Version B excludes matching tests and series. Version C consists of 6 visuospatial tests including sequencing and body image, and 2 matching.

The score for the subtest was most closely related to the total score in version B, and this was also rated the most acceptable version by the therapists. The study by Jesshope *et al.* (1991) showed a correlation between scores on the PBAB and on the ADL score at discharge in 101 stroke patients aged 33–92 years.

8.3.2 The Chessington Occupational Therapy Neurological Assessment Battery (COTNAB)
(Tyerman, Tyerman, Howard & Hadfield, 1986)

The COTNAB is a comprehensive assessment of neurological function for use in occupational therapy. The battery covers a wider area of abilities than the RPAB, and it was designed for use with both stroke and head injured patients. The battery was standardized on 100 head-injured and 50 stroke patients aged 16 to 65 years, with 50 normal controls matched for age.

The battery is divided into four sections, with three tests in each section.

- *Section 1* Visual perception – assesses form constancy, figure ground and logical sequencing.
- *Section 2* Constructional ability – assesses two dimensional and three dimensional construction.
- *Section 3* Sensory-motor ability – assesses sensory discrimination, dexterity and coordination.
- *Section 4* Ability to follow instructions – includes written, visual and spoken instructions.

A comparison of the RPAB and COTNAB was made with a group of sixteen closed-head injury and sixteen stroke patients (Sloan *et al.*,

1991). The average time taken to administer the RPAB was 49 minutes, compared with 80 minutes for the COTNAB. The extra time needed for the COTNAB was outweighed by the additional information obtained in the areas not covered by the RPAB. The patients' subjective rating of the tests showed no preference for one of the batteries compared with the other.

8.3.3 The Rivermead Behavioural Memory Test (RBMT)
(Wilson, Cockburn & Baddeley, 1991)

The RBMT was devised to assess everyday memory in eleven subtests which cover verbal, visual and visuospatial memory. The selection of the tests was based on the memory deficits reported by head injured patients, and the memory problems observed in a rehabilitation setting.

The standardized scores for the battery of tests allow categorization into normal, poor memory, moderately impaired and severely impaired memory. The test was originally standardized for the age range 16 to 69 years, and this has now been extended for 70 years and over.

In one standard score, each subtest is scored on pass or fail. A second standard profile score identifies performance on individual parts of the battery on a scale of 2 (perfect performance), 1 (single error) or 0 (more than one error).

Tests of semantic memory include recall of name, date, orientation, and recognition of pictures and faces. The ability to recall a short story, a route and a hidden belonging are tested, as well as prospective memory for an appointment. The effect of delayed recall can also be assessed by repetition of some tests 20–25 minutes later.

Scores on the RBMT can be affected by an additional perceptual deficit, particularly remembering a route, and recognizing objects and faces. In a study of performance on the RBMT comparing patients with and without perceptual deficits (Cockburn *et al.*, 1990), no difference was found in the two groups in recognizing objects. This was probably due to the use of verbal memory in naming the objects, rather than visual memory. The authors, however, concluded that a shortened version of the RBMT should be used for patients who are unable to complete all the subtests due to perceptual deficits.

8.3.4 The Behavioural Inattention Test (BIT)
(Wilson, Cockburn & Halligan, 1987)

The Behavioural Inattention Test was devised to measure unilateral visual neglect. There are fifteen subtests divided into two sections. Six conventional pencil and paper tests include cancellation, line bisection, figure/shape copying and representational drawing. Nine behavioural subtests relate to daily living situations, such as telephone-dialling, reading the newspaper, telling the time, menu-reading and address-copying.

The test was validated on 125 patients, aged 19 to 83 years, with unilateral cerebral lesions, and showing persistent neglect behaviour at two months post stroke.

Halligan, Cockburn & Wilson (1991) compared performance on the Behavioural Inattention Test with clinical observations made by occupational therapists, in a study of 30 patients with neglect and 50 non-neglect stroke patients. A good correlation was found between BIT and ADL scores, showing that the BIT is ;able to predict those patients who are likely to experience functional problems. The behavioural tests are short and easy to administer. They can be used to identify particular areas that need further investigation in the environment of the individual patient.

8.4 Perception and cognition in functional assessment

The functional approach to assessment plays a major role in treatment in occupational therapy. The aim of functional assessment is to find out where the patient's problems lie, and also whether the patient is aware of them. Some brain-damaged patients deny that they have any difficulties, particularly when these are related to perception and cognition. A patient with neurological impairment may not be able to complete the standardized tests due to poor upper limb dexterity, poor vision, comprehension difficulties or short attention span. Then functional assessment is the only option available.

8.4.1 Task analysis

The breakdown of tasks into stages for assessment and treatment is basic practice in occupational therapy. It is usually easy to observe poor task performance due to physical problems, but perceptual problems are often hidden. The inclusion of perceptual and cognitive components in functional assessments depends on the therapist's understanding of these components in normal function.

There are several overall cognitive requirements for all tasks which include:

- orientation and planning at the start,
- problem solving and monitoring during the progress,
- judgement when the task is completed.

Table 8.1   Activity analysis.

(1) Buying a newspaper		
Activity analysis	Perceptual components	Cognitive components
Find the shop	topographical orientation visual recognition	planning memory problem solve
Enter shop, find, open and shut door	object recognition spatial perception body scheme	attention memory judgement
Locate and select paper	spatial perception figure ground form constancy object recognition	attention memory decision and judgement
Take paper to cash desk	topographical orientation body scheme object recognition	attention problem solve
Pay for the paper	stereognosis body scheme depth perception	memory problem solve judgement

(2) Making toast (early stages of the task)		
Activity analysis	Perceptual components	Cognitive components
Locate bread	spatial perception figure ground form constancy object recognition	planning memory attention
Open packet	spatial perception constructional praxis body scheme	attention problem solve judgement
Select number of slices, put in toaster	tactile discrimination body scheme spatial perception object recognition	decision and judgement

Activity

Choose another activity, for example using a photocopier, playing snooker, and do an activity analysis in the same way.

Sequencing is part of task performance, and the stages must be completed in a particular order to achieve the goal. For example, in driving turning on the ignition, engaging the gear, and removing the brake, must all be completed before pressing the accelerator. However, there are options in the sequencing of the stages in some self-care or work tasks, and the former habits of the individual patient must be considered. For example, in dressing, a patient may begin with vest, pants or socks.

An analysis of the perceptual and cognitive components of the task forms a useful preparation for a functional assessment. The results of the assessment of several different tasks can be compared to find consistent errors that are related to a deficit in one perceptual or cognitive function. For example, problems in dressing and in kitchen activities may originate in a deficit in some component of visual perception.

Two activities are analysed for the perceptual and cognitive components of each stage in the task in Table 8.1.

8.4.2 Questionnaires

The assessment of function in the home environment over an extended period by a questionnaire can reveal realistic information that is not accessible in other ways. This is particularly true in the assessment of attention and memory. The family or carer is in a unique position to observe a patient's problems.

Staples (1991) describes a questionnaire as a 'standardized list of questions, the order and wording of which have been carefully planned', p. 259. Questionnaires can be in the form of a semi-structured interview by the therapist. The results can be used to develop a therapist or carer check-list for the assessment of the patient's behaviour on different occasions, and in different environments, over time.

Self-report questionnaires, to be completed by the patient and/or carer, are easy to administer and demand less of the therapist's time. The questions must be matched to the client's ability to recall information, and to discriminate differences in his/her own behaviour. Reports from the carers are important when the patient is unaware that functional problems exist.

Questionnaires must be designed to give reliable and repeatable information. Positively valued responses are likely to increase, and negatively valued ones are likely to decrease over time.

Careful consideration must be given to the use of behavioural rating scales. A three-point scale, for example using 'often', 'occasionally', 'never' may be insensitive to change, while in a seven-point scale it may be difficult to distinguish between the differences in behaviour.

A questionnaire that is a structured interview, or a self-report, is a subjective assessment influenced by factors such as motivation and comprehension. In the functional approach to the assessment of cognitive problems, a questionnaire can be used as a method for the screening of specific problems, and for the continuous monitoring of the effects of deficits on everyday life.

Summary

(1) Assessment forms part of all the stages of the treatment process, from the early stage of observation to the evaluation of the outcome of treatment.

(2) Standardized test batteries provide objective and reliable measures of the components of perception and cognition, which can be used to predict functional problems.

(3) A pre-assessment analysis of the perceptual and cognitive components of a task can facilitate the identification of perceptual and cognitive deficits in functional assessments. The assessment of cognitive skills should be considered together with physical and visual perceptual function (Abreu & Toglia, 1987).

(4) Questionnaires can provide information about the cognitive problems experienced in everyday life to identify where support is needed, and who will provide it.

References

Abreu, B.C. & Toglia, J.P. (1987) Cognitive rehabilitation: a model for occupational therapy. *American Journal of Occupational Therapy*, **41**, 439–48.

Adams, J. (1991) *The assessment and treatment of patients with perceptual and cognitive dysfunction*. C.O.T. Post Registration Certificate, College of Therapists, London.

Cockburn, J., Bhavnani, G., Whiting, S. & Lincoln, N.B. (1982) Normal performance on some tests of perception in adults. *British Journal of Occupational Therapy*, **45 (2)**, 67– 8.

Cockburn, J., Wilson, B.A., Baddeley, A.D. & Hiorns, R. (1990) Assessing everyday memory in patients with perceptual deficits. *Clinical Rehabilitation*, **4**, 129– 35.

Edmans, J. & Lincoln, N.B. (1987) The frequency of perceptual deficits after stroke. *Clinical Rehabilitation*, **1**, 273–81.

Halligan, P.W., Cockburn, J. & Wilson, B.A. (1991) The behavioural assessment of visual neglect. *Neuropsychological Rehabilitation*, **1**, 5–32.

Jesshope, H.J., Clark, M.S. & Smith, D.S. (1991). The RPAB: its application to stroke-patients and relationship with function. *Clinical Rehabilitation*, **5**, 115–22.

Lincoln, N.B. & Edmans, J.A. (1989) A shortened version of the Rivermead Perceptual Assessment Battery. *Clinical Rehabilitation*, **3**, 199–204.

Nelson, H.E. (1982) The National Adult Reading Test. NFER- Nelson, Windsor.

Sloan, R.L., Downie, C., Hornby, J. & Pentland, B. (1991) Routine screening of brain damaged patients: a comparison of the Rivermead Perceptual Assessment Battery and the Chessington Occupational Therapy Neurological Assessment Battery. *Clinical Rehabilitation*, **5**, 265–72.

Staples, D. (1991) Symposium on methodology: questionnaires. *Clinical Rehabilitation*, **5**, 259–64.

Tyerman, R. Tyerman, A., Howard, P. & Hadfield, C. (1986) *The Chessington Occupational Therapy Neurological Assessment Battery*. Nottingham Rehab.

Whiting, S., Lincoln, N.B., Bhavnani, G. & Cockburn, J. (1985) *The Rivermead Perceptual Assessment Battery*. NFER-NELSON, Windsor.

Wilson, B.A., Cockburn, J. & Baddeley, A.D. (1991) *The Rivermead Behavioural Memory Battery*. Thames Valley Test Company, Bury St. Edmunds.

Wilson, B.A., Cockburn, J. & Halligan, P.W. (1987) *Behavioural Inattention Test*. Thames Valley Test Company, Bury St. Edmunds.

Chapter 9 Visual Perceptual Deficits and Agnosia

The patient with visual perceptual deficits is often unaware of any problem. Function is below the expected levels, even though there may be no sensory loss or muscle weakness. Lorenze & Cancro (1962) were the first to recognize a relationship between disturbance of visual perception and performance in activities of daily living in left hemiplegic patients.

When objects are only partially exposed to view, or are seen from unusual angles, patients with visual perceptual problems have difficulty in recognizing them (Bechinger & Tallis, 1986). The importance of visual perception for effective performance and, more crucially, for safety, was identified by Diller & Weinberg (1970).

The stroke patient with a posterior lesion is most likely to show impairment of visual perception. The assessment of visual perception may be complicated by double vision in multiple sclerosis, and by poor coordination of eye movements in head injury. Visual perceptual deficits may be underlying both the cognitive problems of Alzheimer's disease, and the motor planning problems of Parkinson's disease.

When a patient experiences poor recognition of familiar objects, tests of basic visual perception can eliminate deficits in early processing in vision. The subsequent assessment of recognition from vision, touch and verbal description will give further information about that individual's recognition problems.

Assessments that are appropriate for use in occupational therapy will be described under the headings of basic visual perception, and the agnosias. Spatial deficits, which are closely linked to visual perception, will be described in Chapter 10, together with a description of visual field and eye movements.

9.1 Deficits in basic visual perception

9.1.1 Colour

Inability to recognize colour, in the absence of retinal defects, is known as *achromatopsia*, or colour agnosia. The patient with colour agnosia is unable to match colours, or sort different shades of the same colour. In its severe form, the visual environment is seen as black, white or grey and this only occurs with bilateral posterior lesions. Some loss of colour discrimination, particularly in the blue end of the spectrum, is common in cerebral lesions (Meadows, 1974). An apparent loss of colour perception in the right hemiplegic patient is more likely to be due to a colour naming problem.

If colour perception is impaired, faces and common objects can usually be recognized from other features, but problems arise in the use of money when bronze and silver coins may appear the same. In sorting out clothes, the patient relies on tactile cues, and cannot colour match or coordinate separate items. There is difficulty in distinguishing foods in jars, and in the selection of items, such as tins of soup or beans, from a shelf in the supermarket. Mistakes are only realized from the smell and the taste of food when the tin is opened.

Assessment

Colour matching (RPAB 3)
Ability to recognize different shades of the same colour in blocks of the same shape.

Four stimulus colours (red, blue, yellow and green) are placed on a sheet. The patient is asked to sort the blocks of different shades of each of the four colours under the corresponding stimulus colour.

9.1.2 Form constancy

Form constancy is the feature of visual perception that allows us to recognize shapes and objects as the same when presented in a variety of conditions. Patients with deficits in form constancy have difficulty in recognizing familiar items or objects when presented in unusual orientations and without a background. As a result, he/she may use the item inappropriately. In dressing, if the garment is upside down or inside out it may not be recognized and pants may be placed over the head.

Size is part of form constancy. The same items seen in different sizes need to be recognized as the same.

Assessment

Form board assessment
This is a useful initial test to confirm that the patient can discriminate shape.

The patient is asked to fit coloured wooden shapes of different form into corresponding shapes on the board.

Fig. 9.1 Assessment of shape perception using a form board.

Object matching (RPAB 2)
Ability to match real objects by shape. Colour is constant. Toothbrush, matchbox, car, cup, comb.

Size recognition (RPAB 4)
Ability to recognize and match objects in two dimensions when presented in different size.

Picture cards of the following objects are used: clock, shoe, house, hat and easy chair.

Each object is present in a large and a small version on separate cards. The patient is asked to pick out pairs of the same object from the cards laid out in front of him or her.

Overlapping figures (COTNAB Section 1, Test I)
Ability to match shapes to the components of a complex design containing the shapes overlapping and in different orientation.

A set of five shape cards contains a number of outline shapes on an A4 size sheet. A set of design cards contains complex figures made from corresponding shapes overlapping on an A5 size sheet.

The patient is asked to point to a shape on the shape card, and then to the corresponding shape on the complex design card.

9.1.3 *Figure ground*

Deficits in the perception of figure ground mean that objects cannot be isolated from the surfaces on which they are lying, and from other objects which overlap them. The patient has difficulty in finding things. He/she cannot find the soap in the bathroom, a comb in a drawer, or a cup in a cupboard. In dressing, items of clothing cannot be isolated from the bedcover on which they are lying, especially a white vest lying on a white sheet.

Inability to discriminate figure ground can be observed in the following:

- *Dressing*
  Find a shirt in a pile of clothes.
  Point to the buttons, the sleeve, the collar.
- *Kitchen*
  Find an item in a cupboard.
  Point to an electric socket on the wall.
  Pick out the spoons in a drawer of cutlery.
- *Shopping*
  Select items from the shelf in a supermarket.

Assessment

Figure-ground discrimination (RPAB 8)
A main picture card contains five objects (skittle, anchor, knife, teapot and bottle opener). A pile of ten cards has one object on each,

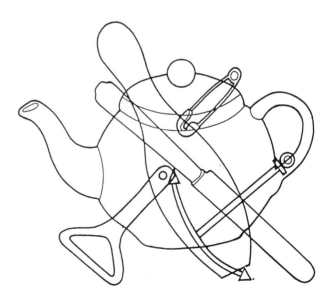

Fig. 9.2 RPAB 8. Figure ground discrimination: main picture card. Extract (not actual size) from Rivermead Perceptual Assessment Battery by permission of NFER-NELSON (all rights reserved).

five of these are present in the main picture card, and five are not present. The patient is asked to decide whether each card in turn is present or not (see Fig. 9.2).

Hidden figures (COTNAB Section 1, Test II)
Five pairs of stimuli are presented. Each pair consists of a simple line figure, and a more complex figure containing the simple line figure. The patient is asked to trace round the simple shape within the complex design using the finger.

Depth perception is part of basic visual perception. This can be assessed by asking the patient to:

● point to common objects laid out on a table in front of the patient, for example, the furthest away, the furthest to the side;
● pour water from a jug into a glass with the unaffected hand;
● walk across busy roads.

Depth perception is part of spatial perception and this is discussed further in Chapter 10.

9.2 Agnosia

Agnosia is the inability to recognize objects and faces. Agnosia means literally 'no knowledge' and pure agnosia is clinically rare. Cases of pure visual object agnosia have been reported and one case study is described in detail by Humphreys & Riddoch (1987).

Agnosia in one modality may be compensated by using others that are unimpaired. A patient with visual agnosia may be able to recognize from touch and proprioception. In tactile agnosia, the patient may be able to recognize objects from vision.

9.2.1 Visual object agnosia

A patient with visual object agnosia has difficulty in recognizing his or her personal possessions, such as the contents of a handbag. There are problems in choosing the right objects in self-care activities, and in selecting items from supermarket shelves when shopping.

An agnosic patient may be able to use familiar objects which he/she cannot name. When presented with an object, the agnosic patient cannot describe its use even when there is no dysphasia. This is different from the patient with memory loss who cannot name objects, but can describe their use.

A left hemiplegic patient (right side lesion) usually has difficulty in forming the complete perceptual analysis of objects, known as apperceptive agnosia. He/she may be able to compensate by handling objects to give additional tactile information, and can be assisted by verbal prompting.

A right hemiplegic patient (left side lesion) may not be able to associate objects with their function (associative agnosia). He/she may have problems in using objects and can be assisted by visual cues.

Assessment

Object matching test (RPAB 2)
This test, described in section 9.1.2, checks object matching before proceeding to object recognition.

Animal halves (object completion – RPAB 6)
Ability to put together two separate parts of familiar animals to complete the whole.

Pictures of five animals (elephant, zebra, hippopotamus, camel and lion) represented as two halves on separate cards, are laid out. The patient is asked to select the two halves that form one animal.

Missing article (object completion – RPAB 7)
Ability to select the missing part of an object. Pictures of five objects with a part missing, and five pictures of the missing parts are laid out. The examples are cat/tail, table/one leg, duck/feet, coat/sleeve and fish/tail.

The patient is asked to match the missing part to the object or animal.

Visual perception (COTNAB Section 1, Test III, Parts 4 and 5)
These tests are aimed primarily at logical sequencing, but they also assess the ability to recognize the same object in different views (egg in egg-cup), and object recognition when only part of the object is seen (battery).

Object recognition (size and viewpoint)
A collection of everyday objects in different sizes, e.g. small and large spoons, screws, and combs, are hidden from the patient. The items are presented randomly in different orientations and the patient is asked to identify each one.

9.2.2 Tactile, auditory and olfactory agnosia

Tactile agnosia or *astereognosis* is the inability to recognize objects by touch in the presence of normal sensation, but with vision occluded.

Patients with tactile agnosia have difficulty when activities have to be done out of view. Doing up a back zip or finding coins in a pocket are examples of this. Work activities using equipment and machines often involve an operation using the fingers without vision.

Assessment

Stereognosis/tactile discrimination (COTNAB (Section 3 Test I)
Ability to recognize objects and textures by touch. There are five objects and five textures for each hand, which are presented in turn inside a box, so that vision is excluded.

Auditory agnosia is the inability to recognize familiar sounds or to distinguish between different sounds. A patient with auditory agnosia does not distinguish the voices of different people. He/she may leave the vacuum cleaner or the TV on, and complain that his/her hearing aid is broken.

If auditory agnosia occurs only on one side, it may be part of unilateral neglect which is described in Chapter 12.

Olfactory agnosia is the inability to recognize familiar smells. The smell of gas, of smoke, and of burnt food is ignored, and this has implications for safety.

9.2.3 Prosopagnosia

Prosopagnosia is the inability to recognize familiar faces. Patients with prosopagnosia are able to identify a face as a face, and know that there is a different between two faces, but cannot recognize who it is. Relatives and close friends may be recognized from their voices and their facial expressions. A patient who cannot recognize his relatives, or learn the names of hospital staff, may have a severe memory problem, or there may be an underlying visual deficit. This requires differential diagnosis.

Assessment

Face matching and recognition
Ability to match and/or recognize photographs of family, hospital staff and famous people.

Pairs of photographs of the people well known to the patient are prepared. The photographs are laid out at random. The patient is asked to pick out the matched faces in turn. Patients without a naming problem are then asked to pick out a named person.

Ability to recognize family and friends in a social environment can also be assessed.

Body (image) scheme (RPAB 10b)
Ability to recognize the parts of a face, and to place them in the correct relationship to one another.

An outline of the head with hair is presented to the patient, and separate facial features (eyebrows, eyes, nose, mouth) are placed below the head. The patient is asked to place the facial features in the correct layout on the outline of the head.

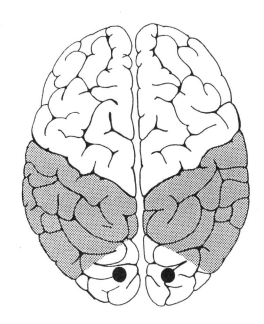

Fig. 9.3 Brain areas associated with visual perceptual deficits and visual agnosia.

9.3 Summary of brain areas

The following summary gives a guide to the brain areas associated with visual perceptual deficits and visual agnosias. Figure 9.3 shows these areas.

- *Occipital lobe* — hemianopia, impairment of shape, size and depth perception.
  (bilateral) — object agnosia, prosopagnosia.
- *Right parietal lobe* — object constancy, apperceptive agnosia, object recognition.
- *Left parieto-temporal junction* — associative agnosia.
- *Occipito-temporal junction* — colour agnosia, object agnosia, prosopagnosia.
- *Temporal lobe* (bilateral) — semantic agnosia.

References

Bechinger, D. & Tallis, R. (1986) Perceptual disorders in neurological disease. Part 1. *British Journal of Occupational Therapy*, Sept., 282–4.

Diller, L. & Weinberg, J. (1970) Evidence of accident-prone behaviour in hemiplegic patients. *Archives of Phys. Med. & Rehabilitation*, **51**, 358–63.

Humphreys, G.W. & Riddoch, M.J. (1987) To see or not to see: a case study of visual agnosia. Lawrence Erlbaum, London.

Lorenze, E. & Cancro, R. (1962) Dysfunction of visual perception with hemiplegia: its relationship to activities of daily living. *Archives of Phys. Med. & Rehab.*, **43**, 514–17.

Meadows, J.C. (1974) Disturbed perception of colours associated with localized cerebral lesion. *Brain*, **97**, 615–32.

Chapter 10 Spatial Deficits

Spatial deficits can originate in basic visual perception, but an impaired spatial component becomes obvious in tasks that require assembling parts together to construct a whole. Performance is also poor when the position of the parts of the body cannot be related to objects in reaching space. Problems in route finding arise when the whole body cannot orient to the layout of far space.

In the assessment of both visual and spatial perception, any background loss of visual field, or poor scanning of space must be borne in mind. In this chapter deficits of spatial perception will be discussed under the headings of scanning, constructional ability, body scheme and topographical orientation. A severe loss of spatial perception involves both near and far space and is known as the spatial relations syndrome. Other spatially related disorders will be considered under constructional apraxia in Chapter 11, and under unilateral neglect in Chapter 12.

10.1 Visual field and scanning defects

10.1.1 Visual field defects

A visual field defect is a partial loss of vision resulting from brain injury, which affects the perception of the space around by limiting the field of view. Visual defects do not originate in the retina of the eye, and they should not be confused with blindness *per se*.

Hemianopia is defined as the loss of half of the visual field in one or both eyes. The term is often erroneously used since there is rarely total loss of half the visual fields. In CVA and head injury there may be loss of variable areas in each visual field, depending on the level and the extent of the disruption of the visual pathway. In multiple sclerosis there may be loss of the central area of the visual field associated with demyelination of the optic nerve.

Some patients develop strategies to overcome visual field defects such as turning the head. Reading often remains a problem. In scanning the page from left to right, the patient with loss of the right visual field cannot make sense of the text after the first few words. The patient with left visual field defect cannot start to read, or has difficulty in picking up the next line as the eyes return to the left.

10.1.2 Scanning defects

A scanning defect is the inability to explore the space around by movements of the eyes, which includes fixation on targets and following moving targets.

Eye movements are impaired by injury to the systems controlling the muscles at the back of the eye. There are several different types of eye movement, controlled by cranial nerve nuclei in the brain stem, and by a small area of the frontal lobe anterior to the motor cortex.

In the head injured patient, the eye movements may become erratic, and random scanning movements lead to delay in interpreting an image. This is less common in hemiplegia. Loss of pursuit eye movements in any or all planes means that the eyes cannot track a moving image. Computer games and many sports activities then become impossible. Poor saccadic eye movements make reading difficult. Loss of coordination in the movements of both eyes to focus on a target may lead to double vision and poor depth perception. Demyelination on the visual pathway may be the source of double vision in multiple sclerosis.

Poor scanning of one side of space should be investigated before the assessment of unilateral neglect.

Assessment

If possible, the patient should be referred for detailed examination of the visual fields using an optometer. Scanning can be investigated by using a small coloured ball and asking the patient to:

Follow the ball as it is moved slowly in different directions – up and down, from left to right, and from right to left.
Fixate on the ball held in one position.

Observation of what the eyes are doing during performance of tasks is also important.

10.2 Constructional deficits

Constructional impairment can be defined as difficulty in the assembly of single units into a two or three-dimensional arrangement. The spatial part of the task is missed.

Many domestic and 'DIY' activities demand constructional ability, for example in the assembly of a vacuum cleaner, food mixer or electric drill. The instructions for assembly need to be visual for the right hemiplegic patient, and verbal for the left hemiplegic patient. Laying the table, putting tops on jars, and decorating a cake all have a spatial component. Constructional ability is part of many work and leisure activities, such as dressmaking and woodwork.

Constructional deficits have been reported in right and left parietal-lobe lesion patients. The errors are related to the spatial or motor bias of the right or left hemisphere respectively. The drawings of a patient with spatial deficits show errors in the relationship of one part or another. For example their drawing of a person may show inaccurate articulation of the limbs to the body. The simple test of asking a patient to draw a person or a clock can reveal useful information to the experienced therapist. For the uninitiated, the exercise only really indicates whether the patient has severe visual neglect of one side of space (see Chapter 12).

The tests for constructional ability are difficult for patients with motor deficits, and the unimpaired limb must be used. Deficits in higher cognitive abilities, such as problem solving, also make complex constructional tasks difficult. Many of the tests do give the opportunity for the observation of other perceptual deficits, such as unilateral neglect and apraxia.

Assessment

RPAB

Test 11   2D right and left copying of shapes.

Test 13   3D copying of a model from component blocks. Figure 10.1 shows 3D copying in the RPAB.

Test 14   Copying a 2D design using cubes.

Fig. 10.1 Assessment of constructional ability using RPAB 13: 3D copying.

COTNAB, Section 2 (constructional ability)
I   2D construction: A – copying shapes. B – draw a clock, a man and a house.
II 3D construction: assemble a 3D model with replica blocks.
III Block printing: copying designs using printing blocks. This test requires the analysis of a complex 2D design, and the selection of the component shapes to construct it in the correct spatial orientation.

COTNAB, Section 4 (ability to follow instructions)
I   Construction of a wire coathanger using a standard jig. The instructions for assembly are written.
II The assembly of a three dimensional construction. The instructions are a series of photographs of the stages.

10.3 Disorders of body image and body scheme

10.3.1 Disorder of body image

Body image disorder is the inability to perceive the appearance of one's own body. It is not a true spatial problem.

Body image is based on the representation of our own body in visual imagery and in visual memory, and it may not be the same as the exact physical appearance of our body. Normal subjects may perceive the hips, or the nose, to be larger than they really are.

Loss of body image is identified when a patient is asked to make a drawing, or to give a verbal description of him/herself. The affected limb may be perceived as very large or very small, known as macro- and micro-somatognosia respectively. The patient may believe that a limb belongs to someone else, often the doctor or the therapist, or give it someone else's name. One patient called his arm George after his son who didn't work! There may be denial of the presence of the affected limb (anosognosia). When asked to move the affected limb, the commands are often ignored, and various reasons are offered as an excuse. Also the patient is liable to injure the affected side.

Anosognosia is seen in right parietal lesions, and may be part of severe unilateral neglect.

10.3.2 Disorder of body scheme

Somatognosia is a failure to perceive how the parts of the body relate to each other, and what are their relative positions in space. It is a spatial disorder of body scheme, which is different from body image.

Body scheme disorder is identified when a patient is asked to assemble a drawing or a model from the parts of the body in the correct relationship to each other. If drawing is difficult, pointing to the body parts on a model, or on the patient's own body can be used.

Confusion of right and left may be part of somatognosia. It is difficult to separate right/left discrimination from other forms of loss of body scheme. In testing, difficulties arise in the transfer of the instructions from the therapist's body to that of the patient, if they are facing each other. Many normal subjects have difficulty in right/left discrimination on body shapes presented in unconventional orientations.

Body scheme is the basis of all movement so that we know where and how the body is moving. The patient with somatognosia has poor balance and equilibrium. Movements are inaccurate, even though proprioception is normal. Self-care activities are difficult for patients with body scheme disorder. A study of a group of stroke patients by Warren (1981) showed a correlation between scores on tests of body scheme and dressing performance. The small number of studies in neuropsychology have suggested that body image disorder is linked to the right parietal lobe, and body scheme disorder to the left parietal lobe.

Assessment

Body image
Drawing a man or a woman forms the representational drawing test of the Behavioural Inattention Test, and the 2D construction test (COTNAB Section 2 Test I).

These tests may give clues to body image problems if the patient is asked to draw him/herself. The representation of a part in an abnormal size, or the omission of a part altogether, may alternatively be the result of motor or other perceptual deficits.

Observations of the patient's behaviour is more likely to give clues to the presence of anosognosia.

Body scheme (RPAB 10a) Assesses body scheme and not body image (shown in Fig. 10.2).

This test assesses the ability to recognize the separate parts of the body, and to assemble them into a whole with correct relationships to each other.

The therapist places the body shape in the centre of the area, and also demonstrates how to place one arm in the correct position. The patient is asked to place the shapes of the other body parts in position.

Fig. 10.2 Assessment of body scheme using RPAB 10a.

Self-identification (RPAB 16)
Ability to copy actions involving the body and crossing the midline.

Touch right shoulder, touch left hip, and so on.

General body scheme assessment
This can be made as follows:

The therapist sits to the side of the patient and asks him/her to:
• point to body parts on command, and by imitation
• move a body part after the therapist has touched it
• touch one part of the body with another part, e.g. 'touch your left ear with your right hand'.

10.4 Topographical disorientation

Topographical disorientation is difficulty in route finding, and the inability to recall the spatial arrangement of familiar surroundings.

Patients with topographical disorientation cannot find their way around the hospital or their own homes. Problems arise in going shopping, and social interaction outside the home is restricted. Similar problems occur in dementia and severe memory loss, so it is important to eliminate these in the diagnosis.

It is useful to try to separate the spatial and the memory aspects of route finding problems. If the patient gets lost because he or she cannot recognize and remember familiar landmarks, the left hemiplegic may be assisted by verbal descriptions of the route with right and left turns. The right hemiplegic may use a map. If the problem is spatial in origin, and right/left discrimination is poor, emphasis on the recognition of landmarks may prove a more successful strategy in rehabilitation.

Most patients with topographical disorientation have other perceptual problems, which may include basic impairment of depth perception, or defective scanning and attention to space.

Assessment

Route finding in the hospital or at home
A route is selected and the patient asked to describe the route in
words (left hemiplegics), or construct a simple map of the route (right
hemiplegics). Then the patient walks round the route, which could be
in a ward, the home, a familiar supermarket (see Fig. 10.3), or in a
workplace.

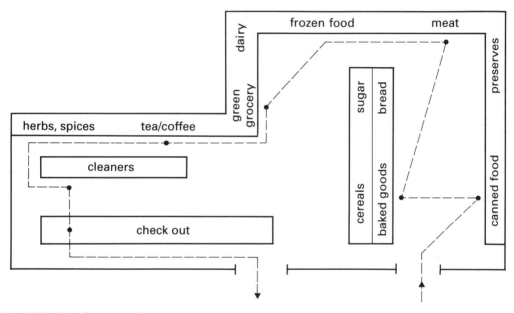

Fig. 10.3 Plan of a supermarket.

Right/left discrimination in a route
The therapist traces a pathway through the simple map used in the
test above, while the patient indicates the direction right or left at
each turn. The same right/left directions are indicated while walking
round the route.

Spatial relations syndrome

Spatial relations syndrome is a severe spatial deficit which includes the
loss of perception of figure ground, form constancy, depth and distance in both near and far space.

The patient may trip up the kerb of pavements, and drop utensils off the edge of working surfaces or tables. There may be difficulty in distinguishing the top, bottom, inside and outside of clothing.

A wheelchair patient may have problems in transferring when he or she cannot judge the distance between the wheelchair and the toilet or the bed. Wheelchair training is very difficult as the patient cannot estimate distances, or turn to the right or the left appropriately. The ambulant patient cannot find the way from one location to another.

A small number of severe cases of spatial relations syndrome have been reported in the literature in patients with bilateral parieto-occipital lesions (De Renzi, 1982).

Assessment

In spatial relations syndrome, the particular problems that affect daily living for the individual patient should be identified. The assessments described in this chapter can then be related to these areas.

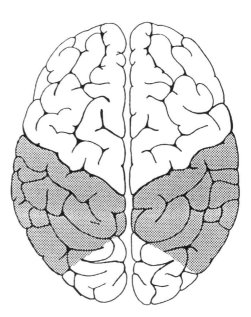

Fig. 10.4   Brain areas associated with spatial deficits in near and far space.

10.5 Summary of brain areas

The following summary gives a guide to the brain areas associated with spatial deficits. Figure 10.4 shows these areas.

- *Right parietal lobe*   – constructional impairment, body image disorder (anosognosia),

                                                       topographical   disorientation,
                                                       spatial relations syndrome.
- *Left parietal lobe*   – body scheme disorder (somatog-
                                                       nosia), topographical disorienta-
                                                       tion.
- *Occipito-parietal* (bilateral)   – spatial relations syndrome.

References

De Renzi, E. (1982) *Disorders of space exploration and cognition.* Wiley, New York.

Warren, M. (1981) Relationship of constructional apraxia and body scheme disorders to dressing performance in adult CVA. *American Journal of Occupational Therapy*, **35**, 431–7.

Chapter 11 The Apraxias

The disorders of movement that originate in the primary motor of sensory areas of the cerebral cortex, in the basal ganglia and in the cerebellum, have clinical features that are broadly related to changes in muscle tone, and to the disruption of action by tremor or by loss of coordination. There are other movement disorders that are not characterized by these features, and they are seen when complex movements are made to command or by imitation. These disorders are grouped together under the general heading of apraxia. No problems of action occur when the apraxic patient is asked to produce simple movements to reach, to point, to grasp, to lift, and so on. Apraxia is seen when simple movements are combined into a sequence to reach a goal.

Three descriptions of apraxia will be given. *Motor apraxia* is observed in a sequence of actions for a specific task using objects. *Constructional apraxia* was originally described as an impairment of the organization of complex actions in space. This type cannot be observed clinically, and it is only apparent on testing for drawing and constructional ability. *Dressing apraxia* is a term that is commonly used for poor dressing performance. It is separated from motor apraxia because dressing includes many perceptual and cognitive abilities.

11.1 Motor apraxia

Motor apraxia is defined as a disorder of movement in the performance of purposeful activities, with the presence of normal muscle tone, normal sensation and good comprehension.

Praxis means movement, and so apraxia literally means 'no movement'. The term dyspraxia is really more appropriate since we are describing a disruption of learned movement, rather than a loss of movement.

Motor apraxia is associated with the upper limb in the use of objects. The same definition can be applied to the movements of the face and lips, and this is known as buccofacial apraxia. There is reason to separate buccofacial and motor apraxia on the grounds of the contribution of the limbic system to the innervation of the facial muscles, whose movements are largely associated with the expression of emotion.

Motor apraxia has been divided into different types based on the identification of different processing deficits and of different lesion sites. Clinically, the separation of ideomotor and ideational types of apraxia provides a useful account of what is seen in patients with cerebral damage.

11.1.1 Ideomotor apraxia

Ideomotor apraxia is defined as a disorder in the planning, timing, and spatial organization of purposeful movement. The patient cannot carry out what is intended, even though the idea is understood. The dyspraxia is seen when the patient is asked to perform movements on command in an unfamiliar setting. There is also difficulty in imitating gestures performed by the therapist.

In the familiar home environment there are no problems with routine tasks that can be completed automatically without conscious awareness. Movements lack fluency and clumsiness is often a source of irritation to the patient and his or her family.

Perseveration of action is common in ideomotor type apraxia, particularly at transition points from one action to another in the sequence. For example, in lighting a cooker, perseveration of the action of striking the match may occur before turning on the gas tap.

When asked to gesture object use, the patient with ideomotor apraxia may use a body part as the missing object. For example, a finger may be used as a toothbrush and rubbed against the teeth demonstrating the actions for brushing the teeth.

Ideomotor apraxia is the most common type seen by occupational therapists. In the absence of other problems, the patient can function reasonably well at home, but safety is at risk.

11.2.1 Ideational apraxia

Ideational apraxia is defined as a disorder in the performance of purposeful movement due to a loss of the concept of movement. The patient cannot carry out activities using objects and tools automatically or on command. Ideational apraxic patients may be able to name and to describe the function of objects, but cannot integrate this knowledge with semantic (conceptual) knowledge of the actions related to their use.

Single actions, such as putting a plug into a socket, or turning on a tap, are done fluently and accurately in familiar surroundings. When there are several actions in a sequence, the elements are not put together in the right order, particularly when more than one object is used. Critical steps in the sequence may be omitted, and there may be a mismatch between object and function. An apraxic patient described by Miller (1986) attempted to pour himself a drink of orange squash by first pouring without unscrewing the top of the bottle, then continuing to pour with the cap removed, and finally emptying it into the water jug instead of the glass.

In testing dyspraxic patients away from their normal surroundings, the ideational dyspraxic may perform a recognizable action which is inappropriate for the object presented. When given a pencil, the movements performed may be those for combing the hair.

Some ideational dyspraxic patients are unaware of the errors they

Table 11.1   Clinical features of motor apraxia.

Ideational apraxia

---

(1)   Single actions for daily living in familiar surroundings are normal.

(2)   Problems in daily living when an activity has a sequence of actions, and/or several objects are used.

(3)   Parts of a sequence of actions may be done in the wrong order, with some omissions, or with two or more parts blended.

(4)   In test situation:
    (a)   can imitate actions
    (b)   incorrect matching of object and action, e.g. brush teeth with comb
    (c)   movements may stop before the activity is completed.

Ideomotor apraxia

---

(1)   Can function in familiar environment at home, but movements are clumsy and lack fluency.

(2)   Performance is not affected by the use of several objects in a sequence.

(3)   Movement may be interrupted by perseveration of an action.

(4)   In test situation:
    (a)   poor at miming actions, less impaired when the object is present
    (b)   body part may be used as an object
    (c)   may also move other body parts (head or body), or vocalize.

are making and are in danger of causing accidents, such as leaving gas unlit in the cooker by the omission of lighting the match. In other cases, the patient is aware of the errors being made but can do nothing to correct them, and may be wrongly labelled as confused.

Ideational apraxia in isolation and in *severe* form is rare, and is often accompanied by some language impairment. The main features of the two types of apraxia are summarized in Table 11.1.

Assessment

Before an assessment of dyspraxia is made, abnormal tone, paresis, unilateral neglect and hemianopia should all be excluded.

Gesture to command (with and without the object)
The patient is asked to gesture the use of objects that are familiar to him or her. The movements are tested in three different conditions:
(i)   on command: 'show me how you would . . .'
(ii)   by imitation   'show me how you . . . like this'
(iii)   performing the tasks using real objects.

Condition (i) is the most difficult, while the additional input from visual, tactile and proprioceptive sensation makes condition (iii) the easiest.

Matching objects by function
Sets of four objects are selected, in which two objects can have the same function, and the other two are visually similar to the target object. The patient is asked to indicate which object has the same function as the target object, for example:
• target object – screw driver,
• other objects – coin, feather and pencil.
Which objects can be used to turn a screw into wood?

Sequencing
RPAB 9 (sequencing pictures)
COTNAB Section 1, III (sequencing)

These tests assess sequencing in common events together with understanding of picture content. The RPAB test 9 includes a flower sequence (see Fig. 11.1) and a bus stop sequence. The patient is asked to put five cards in the correct order.

Lehmkuhl & Poeck (1981) assessed sequences of action with multiple objects using photographs of the stages. In functional assessments in occupational therapy the patient is given all the objects required to perform a task, as in Fig. 11.2.

Assessment of apraxia is based on the ability to match each single action to the correct object, and to complete the actions in the correct sequence.

Fig. 11.1 RPAB 9: flower sequence. Extract (not actual size) from the Rivermead Perceptual Assessment Battery by permission of NFER-NELSON (all rights reserved).

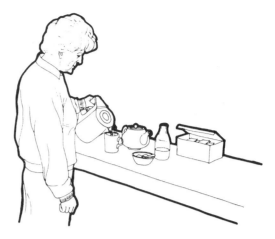

Fig. 11.2 Assessment of sequencing in a task using multiple objects.

Standardized tests of apraxia
There are two standardized tests for apraxia: the Boston Praxis Examination and the Dabul Apraxia Battery for adults used by speech therapists.

The Dabul test is mainly for testing speech apraxia, but does include one test of limb and oral apraxia. Scoring in both batteries is on a four-point scale from normal to inadequate.

11.2 Constructional apraxia

Constructional apraxia is defined as difficulty in the organization of complex actions in space.

The patient with constructional apraxia has difficulty in initiating an action, and perseveration occurs once the movement has started. Many work, domestic and DIY tasks demand the assembly of parts into a unit. Severe constructional apraxia affects all daily living activities (Concha, 1987). It is probably only in sport and craft activities that we are aware of spatial planning.

When single items are put together to form a whole, the spatial relations of the parts must be perceived accurately. Also, the movements must be planned and performed with accuracy to construct the whole.

In a study of a group of 15 right hemisphere CVA patients, Concha (1987) found that performance was at the same level in tests of matching three dimensional designs (spatial only), and in construction tasks where movements were included. Warren (1981) used a two-dimensional copying task to assess constructional apraxia in a group of 101 stroke patients, and no difference in performance was found between right and left hemisphere lesion patients. Baum & Hall

(1981) used two and three-dimensional copying tasks in a group of 37 head-injured patients with multiple lesions. CAT scan data identified patients in the group with mainly right, left, or non-localized lesions, and again no difference was found between them in scores for the constructional test. All these studies show that it is difficult to separate the spatial and constructional components in assessment. This has led to confusion in the definition of constructional apraxia (see Chapter 4).

In the studies by Warren (1981) and Baum & Hall (1981), a clear link was found between constructional apraxia and inability to dress the upper part of the body.

The most likely feature that distinguishes constructional apraxia from visuoperceptual disorders and from other forms of apraxia is a disruption between the visuospatial and the motor planning processes.

The tests for constructional apraxia are the same as those given under constructional ability in Chapter 10. A great deal can be learned from observation of patients performing the tests. The dyspraxic patient will show poor initiation and perseveration during the test. The outcome may be simple solutions, rather than complex ones that require more planning.

Assessment

RPAB
Test 11   2D right and left copying of shapes.
Test 12   2D right and left copying of words.
Test 13   3D copying of a model.
Test 14   Cube copying.

COTNAB, Section 2 (constructional ability)
I   2D construction – copy drawings
II   3D construction – assemble a 3D model with replica blocks
III   Block printing – copying designs using printing blocks.

COTNAB, Section 4
I: Construct a wire coat hanger using a standard jig (Fig. 11.3).

This test can only be used when there is no language problem. Written instructions for the task are graded in presentation and content. The first few stages can be used to assess the integration of spatial and constructional ability.

11.3 Dressing apraxia

Dressing apraxia is a term used broadly to describe the inability to dress oneself.

If it is a true apraxia, the problem lies in the planning of the

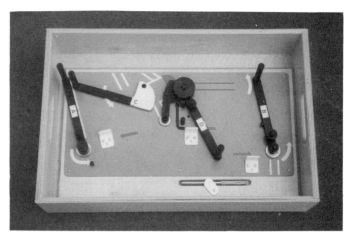

Fig. 11.3   COTNAB, Section 4, I: ability to construct a wire coat hanger using a standard jig, following written instructions. Photograph reproduced with permission from Nottingham Rehab.

movements required in dressing. In reality the activity depends on many perceptual and cognitive functions. Unlike the other apraxias, there is often a rapid improvement in dressing performance with practice in some stroke patients in the early stages of recovery. In other patients, with no significant motor or sensory loss, there is no change in dressing performance after many weeks of practice, and the patient may be discharged without reaching independence in dressing.

Body scheme disorder and constructional apraxia have been identified as contributing to poor dressing performance (Warren, 1981; Baum & Hall, 1981). A breakdown of the task for the individual patient can identify the particular perceptual and cognitive abilities for each stage:

Select garment	colour and form constancy, figure ground.
Orient garment in space	spatial perception, right/left discrimination.
Orient garment to body	body scheme.
Put garment on	constructional praxis, body scheme.
All stages	attention to right and left sides of personal space, sequencing, planning, problem solving and judgement.

Assessment of each of the abilities may identify the stage where intervention will have the greatest effect, and may suggest suitable compensation strategies. Labelling of top/bottom, right/left, will assist problems in spatial relations. Body scheme disorder may respond to verbal strategies associated with limb movements for the left hemiplegic patient (right hemisphere lesion).

Assessment

Tests for the perceptual and cognitive functions listed in the task analysis given above, starting with visual perception and progressing to the higher cognitive abilities.

11.4 Summary of brain areas

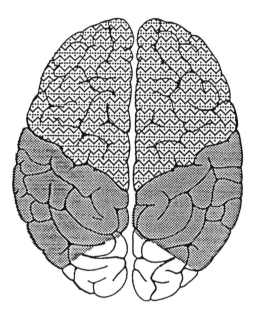

Fig. 11.4 Brain areas associated with the apraxias.

The following summary gives a guide to the brain areas associated with the apraxias. Figure 11.4 shows these areas:

- *Left parietal lobe* – ideational apraxia, ideomotor apraxia, constructional apraxia, dressing apraxia.
- *Right parietal lobe* – constructional apraxia, dressing apraxia.
- *Left frontal lobe* – ideomotor apraxia (right hand).
- *Right frontal lobe* – ideomotor apraxia (left hand).
- *Corpus callosum* – the same as for right frontal lobe.

References

Concha, M.E. (1987) A review of apraxia. *British Journal of Occupational Therapy*, **50** (7), 222–6.
Baum, B. & Hall, K.M. (1981) Relationship between constructional praxis and

dressing in the head injured adult. *American Journal of Occupational Therapy*, **35**, 438–42.

Lehmkuhl, G. & Poeck, K. (1981) Conceptual organization and ideational apraxia. Cortex, **17**, 153–8.

Miller, N. (1986) *Dyspraxia and its management*. Croom Helm, London.

Warren, M. (1981) Relationship of constructional apraxia and body scheme disorders to dressing performance in adult CVA. *American Journal of Occupational Therapy*, **35**, 431–7.

Chapter 12 Disorders of Attention

Disorders of attention can present a major problem in the rehabilitation of the neurologically impaired patient. The close link between memory and attention means that some apparent memory impairment may be due to an underlying attention problem. Poor functional performance in the stroke patient, especially in the early stages in the left hemiplegic patient, is often due to hemi-inattention. Stimuli on the left side of space are ignored. The deficit often resolves in a short period of time, but long-term unilateral neglect has a poor prognosis for rehabilitation.

The head injured patient often shows distractibility and loss of alertness. Fatigue in multiple sclerosis may include the inability to sustain attention, but more sensitive tests need to be developed to confirm this.

Two distinct syndromes will be described in this chapter:

- The neglect syndrome, or the impairment of attention to one side of space, and which overlaps with the spatial deficits included in Chapter 10.
- The dysexecutive syndrome, a disorder of the higher cognitive functions which is associated with frontal lobe damage.

12.1 The neglect syndrome

Neglect is defined as failure to report, respond or orient to stimuli in the space contralateral to the site of brain lesion. The patient is often unaware of the problem, and the neglect may resolve within a few weeks after onset. Some patients, however, continue to show some loss of attention to one side of space for several years (Zarit & Kahn, 1974).

Unilateral neglect must not be confused with a left visual field defect, or with primary sensory loss. Some patients with unilateral visual neglect do have a visual field defect, but others do not. When primary sensation is normal, neglect patients often show extinction to two stimuli, applied one on either side, simultaneously. When both hands or both sides of the face are touched while the eyes are closed, the patient with neglect only reports the stimulus on one side. In visual extinction, if one object is placed in the left visual field, or in the right visual field, it is reported. If two different objects are placed simultaneously, one in each visual field, only the object in the right field is reported.

The loss of orientation and response on one side is not usually complete. It can occur selectively in personal, reaching or locomotor space (see Fig. 4.3).

Some patients show neglect in self-care activities that involve body parts; for example, brushing the hair, shaving or putting on make up. Other patients show neglect when objects are used in reaching space: for example, laying the table, serving tea to several people, or using utensils on both sides of a working surface. Neglect of one side in locomotor space can also be seen when an ambulant or wheelchair patient always follows a route turning to the right, or bumps into things on the left.

Neglect can also occur in different modalities. In auditory neglect the patient does not respond to sounds on the neglected side even though hearing is normal. The patient who does not explore one side of space may have tactile neglect. Other reasons for poor exploration of space on the affected side may be poor visual scanning, or the inability to initiate movements to the opposite side. Loss of body image (anosognosia) may be part of the neglect syndrome when the patient ignores the limbs on the affected side, and may even deny their presence.

Unilateral neglect can affect all self-care, domestic and leisure activities. Poor progress towards independence in self-care alone is a major hurdle in rehabilitation. Less severe forms of neglect affect cooking, entertaining, gardening and social activities. The prospects for return to work are poor.

Two dramatic cases reported are a chess player who failed to use any of the pieces on one side of the board, and an orchestral conductor who ignored all the musicians on one side of the platform (Friedland & Weinstein, 1977). The same authors suggest that affective changes, such as indifference and withdrawal, may also be part of the neglect syndrome.

A questionnaire study of the everyday problems of patients with unilateral neglect showed that patients with neglect did not report more problems than non-neglect patients (Towle & Lincoln, 1991). However, the response from relatives recorded that the neglect patients were having significantly more problems.

Unilateral neglect is most frequently seen in right parietal lesions, but it has also been reported in left parietal lesions. The assessment of unilateral neglect requires detailed observations of behaviour to iden-

Fig. 12.1 Assessment of neglect using a form board.

tify the particular features of the syndrome shown in the individual patient. A check-list of difficulties devised by Bechinger & Tallis (1986) provides a good starting point for assessment in occupational therapy:

- Bumps into things on the affected side
- Hemi-acts – dressing, washing, feeding
- Reads and writes on one half of the page
- Fails to turn to one side and loses way.
- Fails to respond to or notice persons on the affected side.

Clapping behind the back on one side and then the other may identify auditory neglect. The tactile exploration of a textured picture may show neglect of one side.

A form board can be used for early diagnosis of neglect, see Fig. 12.1. The patient has only completed the shapes on the right side of the board. If the shapes are initially distributed on either side of the board, only those on the right will be attempted.

Conventional assessments for unilateral neglect include two-dimensional pencil and paper tests. When the patient is asked to bisect a line, there is a tendency to estimate the midpoint away from the affected side. In cancellation tasks, when the patient is asked to cross out the targets of numbers, letters or words, only those on the unaffected side are marked. In copying, or drawing figures, one side of the outline is omitted, as in Fig. 12.2. The conventional tests are useful in the diagnosis of unilateral neglect.

Behavioural tests use stimuli that are related to real-life situations, for example reading a newspaper or telling the time. Van Deusen (1988) identified the need to relate evaluation tools to functional criteria in unilateral neglect. Behavioural tests can be used to identify possible functional problems, and can be followed up by assessment of the same activities in the patient's own environment.

Fig. 12.2 Copying of a drawing (shown at the top) by two patients with right brain damage (Gainotti *et al.*, 1986, reproduced by permission of Oxford University Press).

Assessment

Line bisection
● Behavioural Inattention Test 5.
Ability to mark the midpoint of three horizontal lines, 204 mm long. One line is across the midline of the page, and the others are displaced to either side of the midline.

● COTNAB, 2D construction, Part C.
Ability to bisect two lines of different length, and mark the centre point of a circle.

Cancellation tasks
The distribution of the errors in the cancellation tasks shows the area of scanning, and the presence or absence of neglect of one side.

● Behavioural Inattention Test 1 (conventional sub-test)
Ability to cross out 40 lines, 25 mm long, distributed over an A4 page, with an equal number on either side of the midline.

● Behavioural Inattention Test 2 (conventional sub-test)
Ability to cross out all the Es and Rs in an array of random letters in five lines, with 34 letters per line.

● Behavioural Inattention Test 3 (conventional sub-test)
Ability to cross out all the small stars in an array containing small and large stars, letters and short words (see Fig. 12.3).

● RPAB 15.
Ability to cross out all the Es in an array of six rows of random letters arranged symmetrically across an A4 sheet.

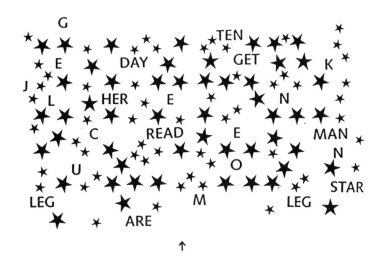

Fig. 12.3 Behavioural Inattention Test 3 (conventional sub-test): star cancellation. Reproduced in reduced size by permission of Thames Valley Test Company.

Right/left copying
● Behavioural Inattention Test 4 (conventional sub-test)
Ability to copy shapes from one side of the page to the other; and to copy shapes presented across the page on to another page.

● RPAB 11 and 12.
Ability to copy shapes and words from one side of the page to the other.
● COTNAB 2D construction, Section 2 Test I.
  ○ copy four shapes
  ○ draw a clock, a man, a house
  ○ bisect lines, mark the centre of a circle.

Behavioural tests
Subtests 1–9 in the Behavioural Inattention Test focus on tasks that are encountered in daily living.

The nine tests include picture scanning, telephone dialling, menu reading, newspaper article reading, telling and setting the time, coin sorting, address and sentence copying, map navigation and card sorting.

12.2 Dysexecutive syndrome (frontal lobe syndrome)

The role of the frontal lobes in the highest level of cognitive function was identified, explored and clearly described by Luria (1973b) in patients with frontal lobe damage.

The advent of computer modelling of cognitive systems has introduced the term executive function, which is analagous to the master programs that control and direct more limited sub-routines in computer technology. Executive functions in the brain include the following:

- goal formation
- planning
- monitoring and regulating
- evaluation of performance.

The impairment of these functions is called *dysexecutive syndrome* or DES which has the following features:

- increased distractibility
- poor monitoring of own performance
- problems in utilizing feed back
- attention and memory deficits.

It has been suggested that the syndrome is the result of loss of the control of attention by the supervisory attention system (see Chapter 6) and of the central executive of working memory (see Chapter 7).

The patient with DES has difficulty in grasping the whole of a complicated state of affairs. He/she is able to work along routine lines, but cannot master new situations. Some of the features of DES are similar to the problems of planning in ideomotor apraxia, see Chapter 11. However, the ideomotor dyspraxic patient can usually function automatically in a familiar environment. The patient with DES, on the other hand, cannot organize him or herself to start an activity.

Many patients with DES have other memory and attention problems. Pure amnesics without DES can still organize themselves by using memory aids, those with DES cannot.

Attentional problems are less obvious when the patient is in hospital or in a rehabilitation centre where there is structure to the day and little need to use initiative or take responsibility. In the late stage of treatment when the patient is discharged to a home environment, the situation changes. It is often the community occupational therapist or the family who identify the problems. Functional assessments in the home may not reveal the true deficits since they are still made in a controlled situation. The role of the assessment of DES is to define a routine for the day, and to identify where structure is needed and who will provide it.

Assessment

Ability to follow instructions (COTNAB, Section 4)
I   Construct a wire coat hanger using a standard jig and working from written instructions.
II   Assemble a three-dimensional construction following a series of photographic instructions.

These tasks demand concentration, reasoning and problem solving. When there is no motor impairment, these tests give the opportunity to observe the level of alertness and the capacity to sustain attention.

Questionnaires and check-lists
Ponsford & Kinsella (1988) devised a rating scale of attentional behaviour in a study of head-injured patients. A 14-point questionnaire was used, divided into three areas of attention – alertness, selective attention, and sustained attention. Each item in the questionnaire was rated on a four-point scale from 'not at all' to 'always'.

Executive functions
This includes evaluation of initiation, planning and organization, mental flexibility, insight and impulsivity, and problem solving.

Methods of evaluation of these higher cognitive functions in the stroke patient are included in Siev, Freishtat & Zoltan (1986), chapter VIII.

Diagnostic tests of frontal lobe lesions
These are used in clinical psychology and include the following three tests:

• Wisconsin Card Sorting Test (Nelson, 1976)
This tests the ability to form concepts and to shift from one concept to another.

• Paced Auditory Serial Addition Task (PASAT) (Gronwall, 1977)
This test is used for the assessment of attention in the head-injured patient. Digits are presented auditorily at a constant rate. The patient is asked to add the first two digits and report the sum, then add the second to the third digit and report the sum, and so on. The digits are presented at a different rate on each of four trials.

• Maze learning is used to observe planning, and modification in response as a result of feedback.

12.3 Summary of brain areas

The brain areas associated with disorders of unilateral neglect and dysexecutive syndrome are shown in Fig. 12.4 and given below:

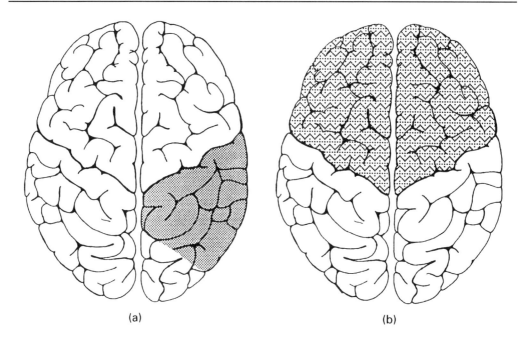

(a)   (b)

Fig. 12.4   Brain areas associated with: (a) unilateral neglect, and (b) dysexecutive syndrome.

- *Right parietal lobe*   – unilateral neglect, anosognosia.
- *Left parietal lobe*   – unilateral neglect.
- *Occipito-parietal temporal junction*   – unilateral neglect.
- *Right temporal lobe*   – unilateral auditory neglect.
- *Frontal lobe*   – dysexecutive syndrome.

References

Neglect syndrome

Bechinger, D. & Tallis, R. (1986) Perceptual disorders in neurological diseases. *British Journal of Occupational Therapy*, Sept., 282–4.

Friedland, R.P. & Weinstein, E.A. (1977) Hemi-attention and hemispheric specialization: introduction and historical review. *Advances in Neurology*, **18**, 1–13. New York, Raven Press.

Gainotti, G., D'Erme, P., Monteleone, D. & Silveri, M.C. (1986) Mechanisms of unilateral spatial neglect in relation to laterality of cerebral lesions. *Brain*, **109**, 599–612.

Towle, D. & Lincoln, N. (1991) Development of a questionnaire for detecting everyday problems in stroke patients with unilateral neglect. *Clinical Rehabilitation*, **5**, 135–40.

Van Deusen, J. (1988) Unilateral neglect: suggestions for research by occupational therapists. *American Journal of Occupational Therapy*, **42**, 441–8.

Zarit, S.H. & Kahn, R.L. (1974) Impairment and adaptation in chronic disabilities: spatial inattention. *Journal of Nervous and Mental Diseases*, **159**, 63–72.

Dysexecutive syndrome

Gronwall, D. & Sampson, H. (1974) The psychological effects of concussion. Oxford University Press/Auckland University Press, Oxford and Auckland.

Luria, A.R. (1973b) *The working brain*. Penguin Press, London.

Nelson, H.E. (1976) A modified card sorting task sensitive to frontal lobe defects. *Cortex*, **12**, 313–24.

Ponsford, J. & Kinsella, G. (1988) Evaluation of a remedial program for attentional deficits following closed head injury. *Journal of clinical and experimental neuropsychology*, **10**, 693–708.

Siev, E., Freishtat, B. & Zoltan, B. (1986) *Perceptual and cognitive dysfunction in the adult stroke patient. A manual for evaluation and treatment*. Slack Inc., USA.

Chapter 13 Memory Problems

Many people with neurological impairment have some form of memory deficit. The effects of any memory loss on function are varied and individual. If the memory deficit occurs with other cognitive impairment, the outcome is even more complex.

For some patients the awareness of memory failures is frustrating for themselves and their family or carers. For others, apparent memory loss may be related to underlying perceptual or attention deficits. The adaptation of the environment to reduce distraction, or the development of strategies to increase alertness, may contribute a significant change to memory function.

Memory deficits make new learning difficult, and this becomes a hurdle in moving to a new home environment where new ways of doing tasks must be learnt. A return to work for the memory impaired person depends on matching the cognitive demands of the work with the spared memory of the individual.

An understanding of the concepts and the levels of processing in normal memory can provide a basis for a structured approach to the assessment of memory loss. In rehabilitation, the assessment of spared memory plays an equal role with that of memory loss.

13.1 Short-term/working memory

A deficit in short-term memory means the loss of the ability to retain and rehearse a small number of items for a short time in memory. This temporary memory system has been most commonly called the short-term or immediate memory. The items that are held may be numbers, words, visual images or ideas. The system is now called working memory (see Chapter 7, under 7.2) but the term has become interchangeable with the term short-term memory in clinical practice.

Deficits in working memory can be modality-specific. Patients may not be able to recall numbers or words that are heard, but can recall them when the same items are seen. Items that are retrieved from long-term memory enter working memory. If a person is asked to describe his/her bedroom, a visual image of the room may be retrieved into working memory and then it is described in words.

Many patients with short-term memory loss cannot hold a conversation. To understand a spoken sentence, a number of words must be held and processed for meaning. In the same way, a number of words retrieved from long-term memory must be held and processed for meaning to produce a comprehensible reply.

Short-term memory is often normal in people with impaired long-term memory. This is the main evidence to support the separation of two broad types of memory with different processing mechanisms. Patients with Korsakoff type amnesia (see Chapter 2, Section 2.3) have a severely impaired long-term memory but they can hold a conversation and they can recall numbers if there is no delay after seeing them.

Assessment

Digit span
A short sequence of numbers is read at the rate of one digit per second. The numbers must be repeated back in the same order. The number of digits in the sequence is increased until errors occur or a maximum of 8 is reached.

Backwards digit span: the same procedure is followed but the numbers are reported in reverse order.

Corsi blocks
Nine black 1½" cubes are fixed in random order to a black board. Each block is numbered for identification. The therapist taps the blocks in a pre-arranged sequence and the patient is asked to copy the tapping pattern. The number of taps is increased by one in succeeding sequences until errors occur. Normal span is about six blocks.

13.2 Long-term memory

Most patients with memory problems have some deficit in long-term memory with normal short-term memory.

The term amnesia is used to describe a global memory loss. In neuropsychology, the amnesic syndrome is described as follows:

- normal short-term memory
- difficulty in learning and remembering new information, known as anterograde amnesia
- loss of some memories acquired before onset, known as retrograde amnesia
- no intellectual or language impairment.

This description applies to some patients after head injury or subarachnoid haemorrhage. In Alzheimer's and Korsakoff's diseases, the deterioration in memory may be gradual, and it is difficult to separate from other cognitive changes. Long-term memory loss is greatest for the time immediately preceding the onset, but some distant memories may be retained. Early studies of patients with severe amnesia reported a selective impairment of semantic (knowledge and facts) and episodic memory for events. Even severe amnesics may have normal language function and intellect, but cannot remember events in the past. This suggested that semantic memory was intact, while episodic memory was impaired.

More recently, studies have been made when the personal semantic memory of the patient was assessed. This would include the names of relatives and close friends from the past, as well as people in films, television programmes, sport or any areas well-known to the patient in the past. Assessment of episodic memory relied on consultation with relatives to provide information about important events throughout the patient's life. The outcome of one study (Kopelman *et al.*, 1989) showed that it is the loss of both personal semantic and autobiographical memory in the recent past, compared with distant past, that is probably the most significant feature of memory impairment after cerebral damage resulting from trauma or haemorrhage.

Semantic memory deficit makes the prospects for employment poor, especially when there is also loss of the ability to learn new information.

Episodic memory deficit means that the patient is unable to remember items coded in time and place, which may be a few minutes or hours or many years before. The patient may not remember what he/she had for breakfast, or that a relative visited the day before. Reading or following a film or television programme may be impossible, since he/she cannot remember what happened a few moments before. The inability to remember events in the past may be distressing for the patient and the family.

Procedural memory loss is rare. Patients with severe loss of semantic and episodic memory can still perform motor skills learnt to a high standard before onset. This means that some work skills, and many former leisure pursuits are still possible. However, memory aids are needed for the parts of the activity that rely on semantic memory, such as keeping the score.

13.2.1 Visual and verbal memory

There is considerable evidence to support the processing of visual and verbal information in different brain areas. Visual and verbal memory can be selectively impaired. The left hemiplegic patient is more likely to have impaired visual memory, and the right hemiplegic may show deficits in verbal memory.

In visual memory deficits, strategies that use verbal memory can be used to compensate, and vice versa. The patient who cannot remember the verbal instructions for a task may be able to follow visual cues and visual prompts. Signs placed around the house to act as prompts or cues can be visual or verbal.

Mnemonics have traditionally been used to aid visual and verbal memory. First-letter cues, rhymes, or a sequence of visual images are examples of mnemonics.

13.2.2 Retrieval problems

In neuropsychology, different theories have been developed to explain amnesia in terms of the inadequate registration, loss of stored memory traces, or the inability to retrieve memories in recall and recognition. There is no single account that explains all memory deficits and recent work suggests that memory impaired people have spared memory that has no awareness, known as implicit memory. More research into normal retrieval processes may develop ways in which implicit memory can be used. Recall is usually worse after a delay, or if there is a distraction. If a patient needs to use information, it needs to be presented as near to the time of recall as possible. Assessment of recall and recognition should always be done in a quiet environment with no distractions.

Retrieval is easier if undertaken in the same environment as learning. This means that practice in one environment does not transfer to another location. Relearning a task in hospital may have no benefit to memory function at home. When questions are asked, the addition of contextual information will assist the memory impaired patient. A question such as 'You saw an occupational therapist this morning, can you remember her name?' is more appropriate that 'What is my name?'

It is the retention of procedural memory that may be exploited in occupational therapy. The identification of a work or leisure skill that has been acquired to a high standard before the onset of memory impairment may restore self-esteem and provide motivation for further memory training.

Assessment

Rivermead Behavioural Memory Test (RBMT)
The following tests assess semantic memory:
1 and 2	First and second name.
5	Picture recognition.
7	Faces.
10 and 11	Orientation and date.

COTNAB, Section 4, III
Ability to follow spoken instructions.

A short story is read aloud to the patient, who is then asked to select 12 picture cards from a total of 25 to illustrate the story. The cards must be placed in the correct order. Figure 13.1 shows the correct cards for the recall of the story.

This test indicates the amount of information that can be retained by the patient, and the recall of early and late events in the story can also be observed.

Autobiographical Memory Interview (AMI) (Kopelman *et al.*, 1989)
This is a semi-structured interview divided into two parts:

● personal semantic schedule – recall of facts from the past
● autobiographical incidents schedule – recall of specific incidents in the patient's past.

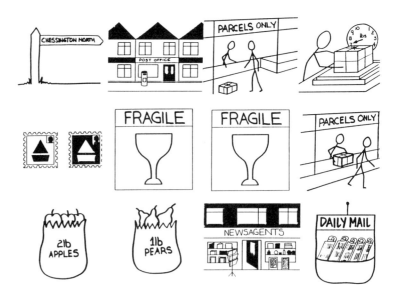

Fig. 13.1 COTNAB, Section 4, III: ability to follow spoken instructions where twelve action cards represent a story. Reproduced in reduced size with permission of Nottingham Rehab.

Three periods of the patient's life are assessed in both parts. The time periods are childhood, early adult life and recent (in the last year). The results give a measure of the pattern of autobiographical memory deficit, i.e. the temporal gradient of retrograde amnesia.

Computer assessment of memory
Computer software is available for the assessment of visual and verbal memory. The number of items in a display can be gradually increased, and either immediate or delayed recall can be tested, see Fig. 13.2.

The value of this method depends on the attitude of the patient to direct interaction with a computer, rather than a therapist.

Fig. 13.2 Assessment of memory using a computer.

13.3 Everyday memory

The way that memory impairment affects function in everyday living depends on the life style of the individual. After cerebral damage, or in degenerative disease that affects memory, the cognitive demands on the patient are changed. Some patients deny that they have a memory problem because their new environment makes few demands on memory.

In occupational therapy, the assessment of independence in daily living tasks may have no value if the patient does not remember to do them. The ability to pursue work and leisure activities may depend on the development of strategies that can be used to overcome specific memory problems.

There is little evidence that memory exercises such as Kim's Game have any value in the rehabilitation of impaired memory. What is more important is to find out what particular strategies can assist the patient to remember what they need to know, whether that is the names of people, or how to transfer to a wheelchair, or how to remember the score at darts or golf. Memory-impaired people will have used a variety of strategies in the past and will need to explore new ones.

The identification of problem areas can lead to the selection of appropriate external memory aids. Alarm watches are effective for some patients but have no value for others. The alarm must be presented near to the point of action, as the patient may forget what to do in a few seconds if he or she is distracted.

Information about the patient's previous lifestyle is an important part of memory assessment. Computerized memory aids will be most successful for patients who have used a personal computer before the onset of memory impairment. Even then, someone else with the time and the concentration must enter the required data, and many memory-impaired patients cannot remember the steps needed to search or clear the data. An alarm with a databank can display a message that gives the action required, for example the Psion Organizer Series 3, seen in Fig. 13.3.

Conventional diaries are more useful for many patients, but only if accompanied by an alarm to remind him/her to read it. Also the patient must be able to relate specific tasks to particular days.

In a study by Wilson (1991), 43 patients were interviewed five to ten years after head injury or subarachnoid haemorrhage. It was found that the use of memory aids had increased, particularly in those who were living independently. Fifty-eight per cent of the patients relied heavily on notebooks, lists and calendars. The author suggested that more teaching in the use of memory aids should be done in the environment in which they will be used.

Fig. 13.3 Psion Organizer, Series 3. The data system can be programmed for messages, and the time system activates a prompt for the message. Photograph from PSION plc.

13.3.1 Questionnaires and check-lists

Objective assessment of everyday memory is difficult to obtain. The use of subjective methods can provide useful information about areas that require adaptation of the environment or the use of external aids.

A questionnaire was developed by Sunderland, Harris & Baddeley (1983), who identified a list of 35 different types of everyday memory error based on interviews with a group of head injury patients. The items in the list were relevant to people leading restricted lives.

The head injury patients were asked to use the check-list for seven days. They recorded which items on the list of memory failures had occurred during each day. The same check-list was completed by a relative, who also recorded the memory failures of the patient over a week. A control group of orthopaedic patients who had suffered trauma without head injury was used. The frequency ratings over a week for each patient were classified on a five-point scale ranging from 'every day' to 'never'.

The most common memory failures recorded were:

- forgetting something you were told a few minutes ago, yesterday or a few days ago
- repeating something you have just said
- unable to follow the thread of a newspaper story
- getting lost on a route you have only been on once or twice.

The results of this and follow-up studies by Sunderland *et al.* (1983) indicate that it is possible for the relatives or carers to draw up a check-list of memory failures for an individual patient. The list can then be used by the therapist to relate the failures to task performance and to develop compensation strategies.

13.3.2 Behavioural observations

The check-list developed by Sunderland *et al.* (1983) has been modified and used by therapists at the Rivermead Rehabilitation Centre to record the memory failures observed in patients during treatment sessions in occupational therapy and in memory groups. The memory check-list included in the RBMT is given in Table 13.1.

The use of a check-list to record memory failures observed by carers and therapists in a variety of settings provides a useful way to identify problems for treatment (Wilson, 1992).

Assessment

Rivermead Behavioural Memory Test
The tests in this battery that specifically assess everyday memory are:
3   hidden belonging
4   appointment

Table 13.1 Memory check-list.

		9.00–10.30	10.45–12.00	13.30–15.00	15.15–16.00

Patient: Department:
Date: Filled in by:

A   Forgetting things: did he/she:

(1) Forget things he/she was told yesterday or a few days ago and have to be reminded of them?

(2) Forget where he/she had put something or lose things around the Department?

(3) Forget where things are normally kept or look for things in the wrong places?

(4) Forget when something had happened, for instance whether it was yesterday or last week?

(5) Forget to take things with him/her or leave things behind and have to go back for them?

(6) Forget to do things he/she said he/she would do?

(7) Forget important details of what he/she had done the day before?

(8) Forget details of his/her daily routine?

(9) Forget a change in his/her daily routine?

(10) Forget the names of people he/she has met before?

B   In conversation, did he/she:

(1) Ramble on about unimportant or irrelevant events?

(2) Find words on 'the tip of the tongue', knowing the word but not quite being able to find it?

(3) Get details of what someone had said confused?

(4) Tell a story or joke he/she has told before?

(5) Forget what he/she had already said, perhaps repeating what he/she had just said or saying 'what was I talking about?'

C   Actions: did you observe the patient:

(1) Having difficulty with picking up a new skill, e.g. playing a game or learning to use a new gadget?

(2) Checking up on whether he/she had done things he/she intended to do?

(3) Getting lost on a journey or in a building where he/she has been before?

(4) Forgetting what he/she was originally doing after becoming distracted by something else?

Number of patients seen in session:
Any other comments or observations:

6 story
8 route
9 message

Subjective Memory Questionnaire
(Bennet-Levy & Powell, 1980)
Forty-three items cover areas including names of people, facts about
known people, films and directions to a known place.

Each item is scored on a 5 point scale from 'very good' to 'very bad',
or from 'very rarely' to 'very often'.

13.4 Summary of brain areas

The brain areas that are associated with particular memory disorders
are the temporal lobe; the diencephalon; and the frontal lobe, see Fig.
13.4.

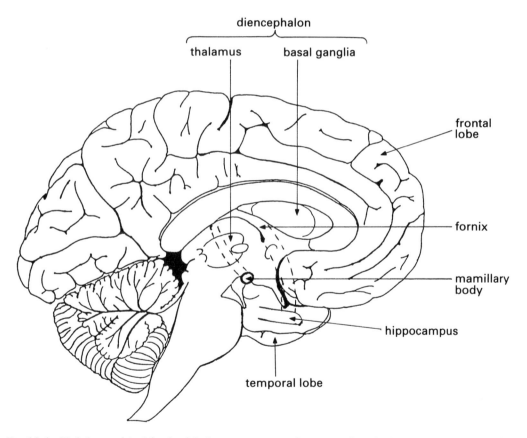

Fig. 13.4 Medial view of the left side of the brain seen in sagittal section to show the brain areas associated with
disorders of memory.

The temporal lobe

The hippocampus is a buried gyrus in the temporal lobe. The importance of the hippocampus in memory was clearly shown in the 1950s when a number of patients in North America were given bilateral temporal lobectomy to relieve severe epilepsy. All the patients developed severe amnesia. Unilateral section of the left temporal lobe led to deficits in verbal memory, and section of the right temporal lobe led to deficits in visual memory.

Lesions in the medial temporal lobe occur in viral encephalitis. These patients experience such rapid forgetting that every few minutes may feel like just waking up. Speaking, walking and other motor or mental skills remain intact, as well as some general knowledge from the past, but memories of recent events may be lost in a few moments.

Tumours of the temporal lobe often produce memory impairment. In head injury, it has been suggested that the medial temporal lobes are particularly vulnerable to damage when the brain is suddenly moved. This may account for the common experience of memory loss after head injury. The extent of the permanent memory loss is related to the length of time in coma and to the period of post traumatic amnesia (PTA) when consciousness is impaired and the patient is confused.

Diencephalon

The diencephalon or 'between brain' is the base of the forebrain that is hidden by the extensive cerebral hemispheres that envelop it. The diencephalon as a whole includes the thalamus, hypothalamus and the basal ganglia. The mamillary bodies that lie in the floor of the lateral ventricle (cavity of the cerebral hemispheres) are also part of the diencephalon. The fornix is a band of white matter that links the hippocampus in the temporal lobe with the mamillary body in the diencephalon.

The two thalami lie on either side of the midline with the slit of the third ventricle between them. Each thalamus is composed of several nuclei that project to the cerebral cortex and the midbrain.

Damage to the dorso-medial nucleus of the thalamus and the mamillary body is seen in Korsakoff's disease. There is severe loss of autobiographical memory in these patients.

Frontal lobe

Damage to the frontal lobe is seen in some head injuries. Atrophy of this brain area, as well as of the diencephalon, is seen in Korsakoff's disease. The memory impairment in frontal lobe damage is usually accompanied by other cognitive changes.

Cerebral vascular accident (CVA)

Cerebral vascular accident, or CVA, may also cause memory disorders. The impairment of memory may be temporary or permanent in sub-arachnoid haemorrhage and cerebral infarct. Deficits in visual and verbal memory are related to right and left side damage respectively. The features of memory loss need to be assessed in the individual patient.

References

Bennett-Levy, J. & Powell, G. (1980). The subjective memory questionnaire (SMQ). An investigation into the self reporting of 'real life' memory skills. *British Journal of Social and Clinical Psychology*, **19**, 177–88.

Kopelman, M. Wilson, B. & Baddeley, A.D. (1989) The autobiographical memory interview: a new assessment of autobiographical and personal semantic memory in amnesic patients. *Journal of Clinical and Experimental Neuropsychology*, **11**, 724–44.

Sunderland, A., Harris, J.E. & Baddeley, A.D. (1983) Do laboratory tests predict everyday memory? A neuropsychological study. *Journal of verbal learning and verbal behaviour*, **22**, 431–57.

Wilson, B.A. (1991) Long-term prognosis of patients with severe memory disorders. *Neuropsychological Rehabilitation*, **1**, 117–34.

Further reading

Wilson, B.A. & Moffat, N. (Eds) (1992) *Clinical management of memory problems*. Chapman & Hall, London.

Appendices

Appendix 1 Blood Supply to the Cerebral Cortex

Three main arteries (anterior, middle and posterior cerebral), and their branches, supply the cortex of the cerebral hemispheres.

A1.1 Anterior cerebral artery

The right and left anterior cerebral arteries lie on the medial side of their respective hemispheres, in the interhemispheric fissure. Each artery passes upwards and posteriorly, passing over the corpus callosum.

The branches of the anterior cerebral artery supply the medial and superior aspects of the frontal and parietal lobes, see Fig. A1.1.

Hemiplegia resulting from occlusion of the main trunk of the anterior cerebral artery mainly affects the lower limbs. Perceptual and

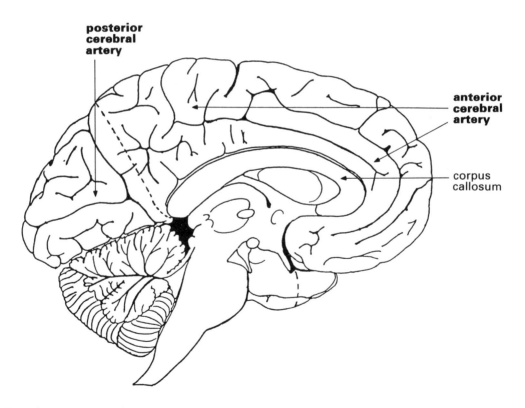

Fig. A1.1 Medial view of the left hemisphere showing areas supplied by the anterior and posterior cerebral arteries.

cognitive deficits may include ideomotor apraxia and dysexecutive syndrome if the frontal lobes are involved, and visuospatial problems if the right parietal lobe is affected.

A1.2 Middle cerebral artery

The right and left middle cerebral arteries are the largest and supply 75% of the blood to the cerebral hemispheres. The middle cerebral artery lies in the region of the lateral sulcus on each hemisphere.

Branches of the middle cerebral artery fan out from the lateral sulcus over the lateral surface of the hemisphere to supply each of the lobes (frontal, parietal, occipital and temporal), Fig A1.2.

Hemiplegia resulting from occlusion of the main trunk of the middle cerebral artery mainly affects the upper limbs and the face. When the left (dominant side) middle cerebral artery is occluded, global aphasia occurs.

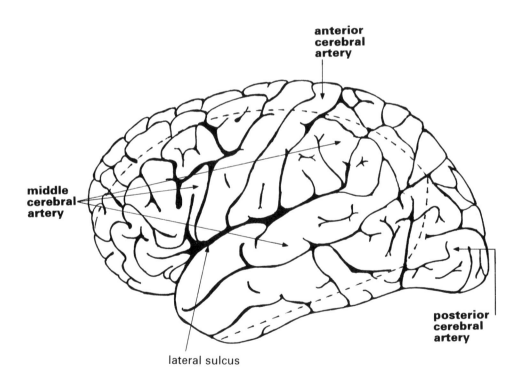

Fig. A1.2 Side view of the left cerebral hemisphere showing the areas supplied by the middle, anterior and posterior cerebral arteries.

A1.3 Posterior cerebral artery

The right and left posterior cerebral arteries emerge between the superior surface of the cerebellum and the medial side of the temporal lobe on each side, and continue on to the inferior surface of the occipital lobes.

Branches of the posterior cerebral artery supply the medial and inferior surfaces of the temporal and occipital lobe, continuing on to part of the lateral surface of these lobes (see Figs A1.1 and A1.2).

Occlusion of one posterior cerebral artery produces homonymous hemianopia of the opposite visual field, and may include colour agnosia and visual agnosia. Bilateral temporal involvement results in amnesia.

Appendix 2 Summary of the Individual Tests in the Standardized Assessment Batteries

A2.1 Rivermead Perceptual Assessment Battery (RPAB)

1. Picture matching
2. Object matching
3. Colour matching
4. Size recognition
5. Series (in size order)
6. Animal halves
7. Missing article
8. Figure ground discrimination
9. Sequencing – pictures
10. Body scheme (image) (a) the body parts of, (b) parts of the face
11. Right/left copying – shapes
12. Right/left copying – words
13. 3D copying
14. Cube copying
15. Cancellation
16. Body scheme – self-identification

A2.2 Chessington Occupational Therapy Neurological Assessment Battery (COTNAB)

Section 1: visual perception

I   Overlapping figures

II Hidden figures

III Sequencing

Section 2: constructional ability

I   2D Construction.

    A.   Copy four shapes – circle, triangle/circle, star, cube

    B.   Draw a clock, a man, a house

    C.   Bisect two lines of different lengths, and mark the centre point of a circle.

II   3D construction

III   Block printing

Section 3: sensory-motor ability

I   Stereognosis and tactile discrimination

II   Dexterity

III   Coordination

Section 4: ability to follow instructions

I   Written instructions

II   Visual instructions

III   Spoken instructions

A2.3 Rivermead Behavioural Memory Test (RBMT)

1.   First name

2.   Second name

3.   Hidden belonging

4.   Appointment

5.   Picture recognition

6.   Story

7.   Faces

8.   Route

9.   Delivering a message

10.   Orientation

11.   Date

A2.4 Behavioural Inattention Test (BIT)

Conventional subtests:

1. Line crossing

2. Letter cancellation

3. Star cancellation

4. Figure and shape copying

5. Line bisection

6. Representational drawing

Behavioural subtests:

1. Picture scanning.
   (i)   a meal on a dish
   (ii) a bathroom sink with toilet items
   (iii) a large window and objects around it in a room (e.g. chair, stool, cupboard)

2. Telephone dialling

3. Menu reading

4. Article reading

5. Telling and setting the time

6. Coin sorting

7. Address and sentence copying

8. Map navigation

9. Card sorting

A2.5 Addresses

The Rivermead Perceptual Assessment Battery can be obtained from:

NFER-NELSON
Darville House
2, Oxford Road East
Windsor
Berks. SL4 1DF

The Chessington Occupational Therapy Neurological Assessment Battery can be obtained from:

Nottingham Rehab Ltd.
Ludlow Hill Road
West Bridgford
Nottingham NG2 6HD

The Rivermead Behavioural Memory Test and the Behavioural Inattention Test are available from:

Thames Valley Test Company
7–9 The Green
Flempton
Bury St Edmunds
Suffolk
IP28 6EL

Appendix 3 Summary of Common Deficits and Lesion Sites

Table A3.1 Summary of common deficits and lesion sites.

Site	Dominant (left)	Non-dominant (right)
Frontal lobe	ideomotor apraxia dysexecutive syndrome memory impairment (verbal) expressive aphasia	ideomotor apraxia dysexecutive syndrome memory impairment (visual)
Parietal lobe	visual agnosia tactile agnosia agraphia somatognosia topographical disorientation constructional apraxia dressing apraxia ideational apraxia	visual agnosia tactile agnosia unilateral neglect anosognosia topographical disorientation constructional apraxia dressing apraxia spatial relations syndrome
Occipital lobe	right hemianopia colour agnosia visual object agnosia alexia	left hemianopia colour agnosia visual object agnosia alexia
Temporal lobe	receptive aphasia amnesia alexia agraphia	unilateral auditory neglect amnesia

Glossary

The prefixes 'a' and 'dys' are used interchangeably in describing deficits. Their literal meanings are 'inability to' and 'impairment of', respectively

achromatopsia inability to recognize colour (in the absence of retinal defects).

affordance possibility for action provided by a surface or an object.

agraphia inability to produce meaningful written words.

alexia reading disorder.

agnosia inability to recognize familiar objects.
> *apperceptive* inability to form the visual percept of an object.
> *associative* inability to integrate object percept with object function and use.
> *semantic* inability to integrate object percept with knowledge of object meaning and function.

algorithm a sequence of step-by-step commands that is guaranteed to lead to the solution of a problem.

amnesia partial or complete loss of memory.
> *amnesic syndrome* global deterioration in memory function due to non-degenerative brain lesion.
> *anterograde* difficulty in remembering new information acquired after brain damage.
> *retrograde* loss of memory for a period of time prior to the onset of brain damage.

anomia inability to name objects and faces.

anosognosia inability to recognize a part of one's own body.

aphasia inability to process spoken language.

apraxia inability to make purposeful movements (in the presence of normal sensation and muscle tone).
> *ideational* loss of the concept of movement (i.e. semantic knowledge related to action).
> *ideomotor* disorder in planning, timing and spatial organization in purposeful movement.

astereognosis inability to recognize objects from touch without vision, (tactile agnosia).

attention selection of the features of the environment for perceptual processing.
> *automatic* attention in habitual action and behaviour without awareness.

controlled   attention in novel situations, or when decision-making is required.
focused   ability to process one input and ignore others.

ballistic movement   action that is pre programmed and cannot be modified once it has begun.
body image   subjective perception of the appearance of one's own body.
body scheme   perception of the relative position of the body parts.
bottom-up processing   analysis of sensory inputs, followed by more complex perceptual analysis.

CAT   computerized axial tomography. A thin fan shaped X-ray beam views a 'slice' of the brain. The X-ray tube revolves round the patient so that the brain is viewed from all angles. A computer combines all the views, and the changes in soft tissue at the lesion site are revealed in a single image.
'cocktail party phenomenon'   the way we attend to some stimuli and ignore others.
closed loop   action that is modified during progress in response to feed back, internal and external.
coding   mental processing of information during learning.
cognitive system   a set of mental operations performed to reach a common goal.
colour constancy   tendency for a colour to look the same under a wide variation of lighting and viewing conditions.
constructional apraxia   difficulty in the organization of complex actions in two or three-dimensional space.
contention scheduling   mechanism for the activation of schema, triggered by the environment, with inhibition of competing schema.
context   the particular circumstances in which an event or action takes place.

declarative memory   long-term memory for facts, incidents and events, that are retrieved by conscious access.
dissociation   the separation of one component of performance that is impaired when others are spared.
dressing apraxia   inability to dress oneself, primarily due to a disorder of body scheme or of motor planning.
dysexecutive syndrome   impairment of executive functions of the brain.

episodic memory   long-term memory for events linked to a time and place.
everyday memory   memory function related to daily living.

executive   'master program' that controls small subprograms.
    central   a component of working memory.
explicit memory   memory processes with awareness, assessed by tests of direct recall and recognition.

figure ground   isolation of a shape or an object from its background.
form constancy   the perception of a familiar shape or object as the same, regardless of its position or the distance from which it is viewed.

gestalt   unified whole that is not revealed by simply analysing the parts.

hemianopia   'blindness' in part of the visual field of one or both eyes.
    homonymous   'blindness' in the right or left side visual fields of both eyes.
hemiplegia   weakness or spasticity in the muscles of one side of the body, resulting from a lesion in the opposite side of the brain.

implicit memory   memory that is not directly observable in tests of recall and recognition.

lesion (brain)   change in the tissue of the brain resulting from vascular accident, trauma, disease or degeneration.
lexicon   store of known words.
long-term memory   stores and processes information over periods of time from a few minutes to many years.

memory trace   neurological processing for a relatively permanent memory.
mnemonic   system designed to aid memory.
modality   a sensory system, e.g. visual modality, tactile modality.
module   a theoretically discrete perceptual or cognitive ability, e.g. colour perception.
MRI   magnetic resonance imaging. A strong magnetic field is produced by electromagnets distributed around the head. A radio pulse excites the hydrogen atoms in the water in the brain tissue. A computer translates the signals from the movement of the hydrogen atoms into an image, which identifies where lesions have occurred.
myelin   fatty sheath around axons of neurones in the white matter of the central nervous system, and in peripheral nerves, which increases the rate of conduction of nerve impulses.

neglect syndrome   failure to orient, report or respond to stimuli on one side of space (contralateral to the side of brain lesion).

object constancy   the tendency for objects to be perceived as the same, even though they are observed in a variety of conditions, e.g. distance, orientation, location or lighting.

object-centred description   representation of the visual structure of an object, irrespective of viewpoint.

object-recognition units   stored visual descriptions of all known objects.

open loop   movement that cannot be modified once it has started, e.g. tap a key, throw a ball.

optic aphasia   inability to name objects when presented visually.

paradigm   a particular experimental procedure.

perseveration   tendency to continue a particular action, word or pattern of behaviour, without any stimulus for it.

procedural memory   long- term memory for mental and motor skills that are retrieved without conscious awareness.

prosopagnosia   inability to recognize familiar faces.

prospective memory   memory for future actions without obvious external cues.

representation   symbolic description that is a momentary pattern of activity in a neural network.
 structural   as it is now.
 stored memory   as it has been in the past.

saccade   a fast eye movement between two fixation points occurring in scanning and reading.

scanning   the exploration of space by eye movements.

scheme-a   a set of rules or procedures developed from past action or behaviour, which acts as plans for future ones.

semantic   related to meaning.

semantic memory   long-term memory for general knowledge and facts.

somatognosia   failure to perceive how the body parts relate to each other, and their relative positions in space (disorder of body scheme).

spatial relations syndrome   a severe spatial deficit in all aspects of spatial perception.

supervisory attention system   system for controlled attention in novel situations, or when decision making is required.

syndrome   a collection of symptoms that commonly occur together.

top-down processing   processes controlled by thoughts or memories about the world which influence the interpretation of information from the senses.

topographical disorientation   inability to recall the spatial arrangement of familiar surroundings.

topographical memory memory for the landmarks and layout of familiar surroundings.

unilateral visual neglect inability to orient to visual stimuli in one side of space.

viewer-centred representation visual representation of an object from the viewpoint of the observer.

visual field area of the visual world that is visible out of the eye.

visuospatial sketch pad processing of visuospatial information in working memory.

working memory temporary storage of visuospatial and acoustic material controlled by an attentional system (central executive).

Index